Forecasting Time Series Data with Facebook Prophet

Build, improve, and optimize time series forecasting models using the advanced forecasting tool

Greg Rafferty

BIRMINGHAM—MUMBAI

Forecasting Time Series Data with Facebook Prophet

Copyright © 2021 Packt Publishing

Group Product Manager: Kunal Parikh

Publishing Product Manager: Sunith Shetty

Senior Editor: Roshan Kumar

Content Development Editor: Tazeen Shaikh

Technical Editor: Manikandan Kurup

Copy Editor: Safis Editing

Project Coordinator: Aishwarya Mohan

Proofreader: Safis Editing

Indexer: Priyanka Dhadke

Production Designer: Jyoti Chauhan

First published: March 2021

Production reference: 1100221

Published by Packt Publishing Ltd.
Livery Place
35 Livery Street
Birmingham
B3 2PB, UK.

ISBN 978-1-80056-853-2

www.packt.com

Contributors

About the author

Greg Rafferty is a data scientist in San Francisco, California. With over a decade of experience, he has worked with many of the top firms in tech, including Google, Facebook, and IBM. Greg has been an instructor in business analytics on Coursera and has led face-to-face workshops with industry professionals in data science and analytics. With both an MBA and a degree in engineering, he is able to work across the spectrum of data science and communicate with both technical experts and non-technical consumers of data alike.

About the reviewers

Jose Angel Sanchez, born and raised in Oaxaca, Mexico, is a software developer at Pinterest. Previously, Jose worked at Bayer, Credijusto, and Connus International, and throughout his career has had the opportunity to work with different technologies, solving problems in different disciplines. A math lover and a crypto-believer, he knows that only through science and skeptical thinking will the human race achieve its true potential. Jose lives happily with his wife, Mariana, and their dog, Koly, in St Louis, Missouri.

Mert Sarıkaya graduated with a double major in industrial engineering and mathematics from Bogazici University and is currently pursuing his master's degree in industrial engineering from Bogazici University, with a focus on time series forecasting. He has worked for a retail analytics company as a machine learning engineer, specializing in demand prediction by using time series data. He is currently working as a data scientist in Algopoly to solve large-scale forecasting problems in the energy and finance sectors. He is a supporter of the open source community and has also made a small contribution to the `fbprophet` library. He is interested in cinema and loves to cook in his free time.

Table of Contents

Section 2:
Seasonality, Tuning, and Advanced Features

3
Non-Daily Data

4
Seasonality

5
Holidays

6
Growth Modes

Technical requirements 115
Applying linear growth 116
Understanding the logistic function 118
Saturating forecasts 119
Increasing logistic growth 121
Non-constant cap 126
Decreasing logistic growth 127
Applying flat growth 130
Summary 134

7
Trend Changepoints

Technical requirements 138
Automatic trend changepoint detection 138
Default changepoint detection 138
Regularizing changepoints 143
Specifying custom changepoint locations 148
Summary 155

8
Additional Regressors

Technical requirements 158
Adding binary regressors 158
Adding continuous regressors 163
Interpreting the regressor coefficients 165
Summary 169

9
Outliers and Special Events

Technical requirements 172
Correcting outliers that cause seasonality swings 172
Correcting outliers that cause wide uncertainty intervals 177
Detecting outliers automatically 180
Winsorizing 181
Standard deviation 182
Moving average 183
Error standard deviation 185
Modeling outliers as special events 188
Summary 191

10
Uncertainty Intervals

Section 3: Diagnostics and Evaluation

11
Cross-Validation

12
Performance Metrics

13
Productionalizing Prophet

Other Books You May Enjoy

Index

Preface

In 2017, Facebook released their Prophet software as open source. This powerful tool was developed by Facebook engineers because their analysts were becoming overwhelmed with the number of business forecasts demanded by managers. The developers of Prophet wanted to simultaneously solve two problems: a) completely automatic forecasting techniques are too brittle and inflexible to handle additional knowledge, and b) analysts who are consistently able to produce high-quality forecasts are rare and require extensive expertise. Prophet successfully solves both of these problems.

Prophet was designed so that forecasts produced with no parameter tuning or other optimization are usually very high quality, but with just a little bit of training, anyone can intuitively tweak the model and increase performance dramatically.

Starting from the most basic model and advancing to the deepest technical dives into Prophet's inner workings, this book will teach you everything there is to know about Facebook's Prophet. Many advanced features not even covered by the official documentation are discussed here, with complete working examples for every topic covered. This book is not intended to provide you the ability to build a Prophet clone from scratch, but it will teach you to use Prophet just as well as, if not better than, Facebook's own highly-trained engineers.

Who this book is for

This book is for anyone who wants to use Facebook's Prophet to improve their forecasts. Data scientists and data analysts, machine learning engineers and software engineers, and even business managers will benefit from the topics covered in this book. All that is required is that the reader is comfortable with working in either Python or R, or is willing to learn how. The business manager who is familiar with Python can follow the examples included in this book and will learn how to modify them to fit their own use cases; the data scientist will gain a more technical understanding of what Prophet is doing under the hood and how it works. However, this book is intended mostly as a *how-to guide*. It will not provide a fully rigorous explanation of the math and statistics that underpin the equations controlling Prophet. For that, I suggest reading the original Prophet paper: *Taylor SJ, Letham B. 2017. Forecasting at scale. PeerJ Preprints 5:e3190v2* (`https://doi.org/10.7287/peerj.preprints.3190v2`).

What this book covers

Chapter 1, The History and Development of Time Series Forecasting, will teach you about the earliest efforts to understand time series data and the main algorithmic developments up to the present day.

Chapter 2, Getting Started with Facebook Prophet, will walk you through the process of getting Prophet running on your machine, and then will test your installation by building your first model.

Chapter 3, Non-Daily Data, will cover how to modify the approach taken in the previous chapter in order to handle data that is recorded on a scale other than daily, so that you will be set up to work through all of the examples in later chapters.

Chapter 4, Seasonality, will discuss all of the ways to control seasonality in Prophet. Seasonality is one of the building blocks of Prophet models and contains the most control parameters, so this chapter is the longest but also one of the most important.

Chapter 5, Holidays, will teach you how to add the effect of holidays to your forecast. You will learn how to include a basic set of default holidays, how to change that set for different regions, how to add your own custom holidays, and how to control the strength of the effect.

Chapter 6, Growth Modes, will describe the three growth modes a trend line in Prophet can follow: linear, logistic, and flat. You will learn which scenarios to apply these modes to and observe what effect they have on your future forecasts.

Chapter 7, Trend Changepoints, will talk about how to control the rigidity of your final model. You will learn how to make a flexible model that can change direction often, or a rigid model that follows a constant line, why you may choose one or the other, and the effect this has on the uncertainty of your model with future data.

Chapter 8, Additional Regressors, will teach you how to include additional columns of data in your model. Similar to multi-variate regression, Prophet is able to combine multiple input vectors in a predictive forecast.

Chapter 9, Outliers and Special Events, will show you the two types of problems that outliers can cause in a Prophet model and will teach you several automated techniques for identifying outliers and how to handle them with Prophet.

Chapter 10, Uncertainty Intervals, will cover how to quantify the uncertainty in your model using different statistical methods, what the benefits and drawbacks of each method are, and how to visualize the amount of risk in your model.

Chapter 11, Cross-Validation, will teach you how to perform cross-validation in Prophet. You may already be familiar with cross-validation techniques in machine learning, but with time series data a different approach is needed. This chapter will teach you that approach and how to implement it in Prophet.

Chapter 12, Performance Metrics, will build upon the previous chapter and introduce the performance metrics Prophet features. You will learn how to combine cross validation with your chosen metric of performance to perform a grid search and optimize your model to gain the highest predictive accuracy.

Chapter 13, Productionalizing Prophet, is the final chapter and will teach you some additional techniques that will come in handy when using Prophet in a production environment. You will learn how to save your models for later use, how to update models as new data comes in, and how to use Prophet's Plotly plot functions to build highly interactive charts suitable for sharing on a web-based dashboard.

To get the most out of this book

To run the code examples in this book, you will need **Python 3.x** installed. All examples in this book were made using Prophet version 0.71 in Jupyter Notebooks. MacOS, Windows, and Linux are all supported. Although all examples in this book will be written in Python, everything is also fully compatible with R and you may use that language if you prefer, although this book will not cover R syntax. Please refer to the official Prophet documentation for R syntax (`https://facebook.github.io/prophet/`).

Chapter 2, Getting Started with Facebook Prophet will walk you through installing Facebook Prophet, and installing either Anaconda or Miniconda is strongly recommended in order to correctly install all of Prophet's dependencies. It is possible to install Prophet without using Anaconda, but it can be very difficult depending upon the specific configuration of your machine, and this book will assume Anaconda will be used.

In order to follow the examples, you must at least be familiar with the `pandas` library for data processing and `Matplotlib` for making plots. In a few cases, the `numpy` library will be used to simulate random data but following the examples will not require that you know the NumPy syntax. All of these libraries will be installed automatically as Prophet dependencies, if not already installed. All datasets are hosted and can be downloaded from this book's GitHub repo here: `https://github.com/PacktPublishing/Forecasting-Time-Series-Data-with-Facebook-Prophet`.

Software/Hardware covered in the book	OS requirements
Facebook Prophet	Windows, Mac OS X, and Linux (Any)

Prophet supports parallelization with **Dask** but, while setting Prophet up to run on a Dask cluster will be covered, installing and using Dask is beyond the scope of this book. Similarly, this book will cover how to build interactive Prophet visualizations in Plotly but putting those together into a Dash dashboard will be left up to the reader to learn elsewhere.

If you are using the digital version of this book, we advise you to type the code yourself or access the code via the GitHub repository (link available in the next section). Doing so will help you avoid any potential errors related to copy/pasting of code.

Download the example code files

You can download the example code files for this book from GitHub at `https://github.com/PacktPublishing/Forecasting-Time-Series-Data-with-Facebook-Prophet`. In case there's an update to the code, it will be updated on the existing GitHub repository.

We also have other code bundles from our rich catalog of books and videos available at `https://github.com/PacktPublishing/`. Check them out!

Download the color images

We also provide a PDF file that has color images of the screenshots/diagrams used in this book. You can download it here: `https://static.packt-cdn.com/downloads/9781800568532_ColorImages.pdf`.

Conventions used

There are a number of text conventions used throughout this book.

`Code in text`: Indicates code words in text, database table names, folder names, filenames, file extensions, pathnames, dummy URLs, user input, and Twitter handles. Here is an example: "The `make_future_dataframe` method requires us to specify the number of days we intend to forecast out."

A block of code is set as follows:

```
model = Prophet()
model.fit(df)
future = model.make_future_dataframe(periods=365)
forecast = model.predict(future)
fig = model.plot(forecast)
plt.show()
```

When we wish to draw your attention to a particular part of a code block, the relevant lines or items are set in bold:

```
model = Prophet()
model.fit(df)
future = model.make_future_dataframe(periods=60, freq='MS')
forecast = model.predict(future)
fig = model.plot(forecast)
plt.show()
```

Any command-line input or output is written as follows:

```
pip install pystan
pip install fbprophet
```

Bold: Indicates a new term, an important word, or words that you see on screen. For example, words in menus or dialog boxes appear in the text like this. Here is an example: "In the following seasonality plot, I've used the **Toggle Spike Lines** and **Compare Data** buttons from this toolbar to add further information to the hover tooltip, seen here:"

> **Tips or important notes**
> Appear like this.

Get in touch

Feedback from our readers is always welcome.

General feedback: If you have questions about any aspect of this book, mention the book title in the subject of your message and email us at customercare@packtpub.com.

Errata: Although we have taken every care to ensure the accuracy of our content, mistakes do happen. If you have found a mistake in this book, we would be grateful if you would report this to us. Please visit www.packtpub.com/support/errata, selecting your book, clicking on the Errata Submission Form link, and entering the details.

Piracy: If you come across any illegal copies of our works in any form on the Internet, we would be grateful if you would provide us with the location address or website name. Please contact us at copyright@packt.com with a link to the material.

If you are interested in becoming an author: If there is a topic that you have expertise in and you are interested in either writing or contributing to a book, please visit authors.packtpub.com.

Reviews

Please leave a review. Once you have read and used this book, why not leave a review on the site that you purchased it from? Potential readers can then see and use your unbiased opinion to make purchase decisions, we at Packt can understand what you think about our products, and our authors can see your feedback on their book. Thank you!

For more information about Packt, please visit packt.com.

Section 1: Getting Started

The first part of this book will give you an understanding of the historical developments in time series forecasting techniques that led to the inception of Prophet and then guide you through the installation of the program. The section closes with a walk-through of a basic Prophet forecasting model and introduces the output that such a model produces.

This section comprises the following chapters:

- *Chapter 1, The History and Development of Time Series Forecasting*
- *Chapter 2, Getting Started with Facebook Prophet*

1
The History and Development of Time Series Forecasting

Facebook Prophet is a powerful tool for creating, visualizing, and optimizing your forecasts! With Prophet, you'll be able to understand what factors will drive your future results and enable you to make more confident decisions. You'll accomplish these tasks and goals through an intuitive but very flexible programming interface that is designed for both the beginner and expert alike.

You don't need a deep knowledge of the math or statistics behind time series forecasting techniques to leverage the power of Prophet, although if you do possess this knowledge, Prophet includes a rich feature set that allows you to deploy your experience to great effect. You'll be working in a structured paradigm where each problem follows the same pattern, allowing you to spend less time figuring out how to optimize your forecast and more time discovering key insights to supercharge your decisions.

This chapter introduces the foundational ideas behind time series forecasting and discusses some of the key model iterations that eventually led to the development of Prophet. In this chapter, you'll learn what time series data is and why it must be handled differently than non-time series data, and then you'll discover the most powerful innovations, of which Prophet is the latest. Specifically, we will cover an overview of what time series forecasting is and then go into more detail on some specific approaches:

- Understanding time series forecasting
- Moving average and exponential smoothing
- ARIMA
- ARCH/GARCH
- Neural networks
- Prophet

Understanding time series forecasting

A **time series** is a set of data collected sequentially over time. For example, think of any chart where the *x*-axis is some measurement of time—anything from the number of stars in the Universe since the Big Bang until today or the amount of energy released each nanosecond of a nuclear reaction. The data behind both are time series. The chart in the weather app on your phone showing the expected temperature for the next 7 days? That's also the plot of a time series.

In this book, we are mostly concerned with events on the human scales of years, months, days, and hours, but all of this is time series data. Predicting future values is the act of forecasting.

Forecasting the weather has obviously been important to humans for millennia, particularly since the advent of agriculture. In fact, over 2,300 years ago, the Greek philosopher Aristotle wrote a treatise called *Meteorology* that contained a discussion of early weather forecasting. The very word *forecast* was coined by an English meteorologist in the 1850s, Robert FitzRoy, who achieved fame as the captain of the *HMS Beagle* during Charles Darwin's pioneering voyage.

But time series data is not unique to weather. The field of medicine adopted time series analysis techniques with the 1901 invention of the first practical electrocardiogram by the Dutch physician Willem Einthoven. The **ECG**, as it is commonly known, produces the familiar pattern of heartbeats we now see on the machine next to a patient's bed in every medical drama.

Today, one of the most discussed fields of forecasting is economics. There are entire television channels dedicated to analyzing trends of the stock market. Governments use economic forecasting to advise central bank policy, politicians use economic forecasting to develop their platforms, and business leaders use economic forecasting to guide their decisions.

In this book, we will be forecasting topics as varied as carbon dioxide levels high in the atmosphere, the number of riders on Chicago's public bike share program, the growth of the wolf population in Yellowstone, the solar sunspot cycles, local rainfall, and even Instagram likes on some popular accounts.

The problem with dependent data

So, why does time series forecasting require its own unique approach? From a statistical perspective, you might see a scatter plot of time series with a relatively clear trend and attempt to fit a line using standard regression—the technique for fitting a straight line through data. The problem is that this violates the assumption of independence that linear regression demands.

To illustrate time series dependence with an example, let's say that a gambler is rolling an unbiased die. I tell you that he just rolled a 2 and ask what the next value will be. This data is independent; previous rolls have no effect on future rolls, so knowing that the previous roll was a 2 does not provide any information about the next roll.

However, in a different situation, let's say that I call you from an undisclosed location somewhere on Earth and ask you to guess the temperature at my location. Your best bet would be to guess some average global temperature for that day. But now, imagine that I tell you that yesterday's temperature at my location was 90°F. That provides a great deal of information to you because you intuitively know that yesterday's temperature and today's temperature are linked in some way; they are not independent.

With time series data, you cannot randomly shuffle the order of data around without disturbing the trends, within a reasonable margin of error. The order of the data matters; it is not independent. When data is dependent like this, a regression model can show statistical significance by random chance, even when there is no true correlation, much more often than your chosen confidence level would suggest.

Because high values tend to follow high values and low values tend to follow low values, a time series dataset is more likely to show more clusters of high or low values than would otherwise be present, and this in turn can lead to the appearance of more correlations than would otherwise be present.

The website *Spurious Correlations* by Tyler Vigen specializes in pointing out examples of seemingly significant, but utterly ridiculous, time series correlations. Here is one example:

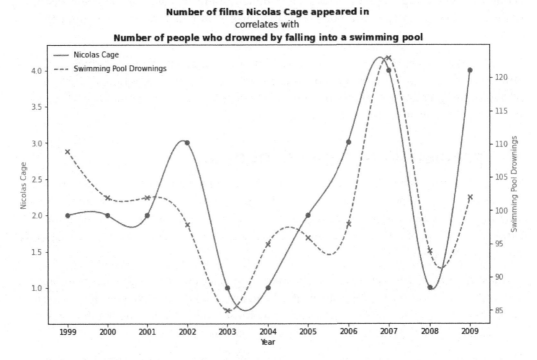

Figure 1.1 – A spurious time series correlation. https://www.tylervigen.com/spurious-correlations

Obviously, the number of people who drown in pools each year is completely independent of the number of films Nicolas Cage appears in. They simply have no effect on each other at all. However, by making the fallacy of treating time series data as if it were independent, Vigen has shown that by pure random chance, the two series of data do, in fact, correlate significantly. These types of random chances are much more likely to happen when ignoring the dependence of time series data.

Now that you understand what exactly time series data is and what sets it apart from other datasets, let's look at a few milestones in the development of models, from the earliest models up to Prophet.

Moving average and exponential smoothing

Possibly the simplest form of forecasting is the **moving average**. Often, a moving average is used as a **smoothing technique** to find a straighter line through data with a lot of variation. Each data point is adjusted to the value of the average of n surrounding data points, with n being referred to as the window size. With a window size of 10, for example, we would adjust a data point to be the average of the 5 values before and the 5 values after. In a forecasting setting, the future values are calculated as the average of the n previous values, so again, with a window size of 10, this means the average of the 10 previous values.

The balancing act with a moving average is that you want a large window size in order to smooth out the noise and capture the actual trend, but with a larger window size, your forecasts are going to lag the trend significantly as you reach back further and further to calculate the average. The idea behind **exponential smoothing** is to apply exponentially decreasing weights to the values being averaged over time, giving recent values more weight and older values less. This allows the forecast to be more reactive to changes, while still ignoring a good deal of noise.

As you can see in the following plot of simulated data, the moving average line exhibits much rougher behavior than the exponential smoothing line, but both lines still adjust to trend changes at the same time:

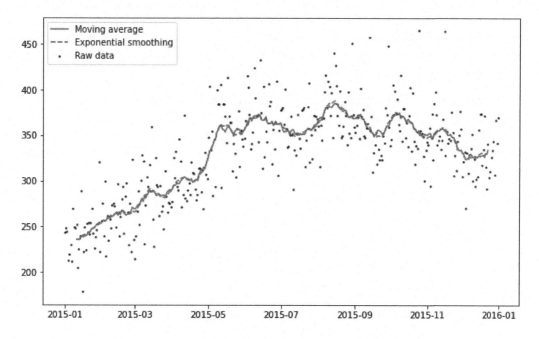

Figure 1.2 – Moving average versus exponential smoothing

Exponential smoothing originated in the 1950s with **simple exponential smoothing**, which does not allow for a trend or seasonality. Charles Holt advanced the technique in 1957 to allow for a trend with what he called **double exponential smoothing**; and in collaboration with Peter Winters, Holt added seasonality support in 1960, in what is commonly called **Holt-Winters exponential smoothing**.

The downside to these methods of forecasting is that they can be slow to adjust to new trends and so forecasted values lag behind reality—they do not hold up well to longer forecasting timeframes, and there are many hyperparameters to tune, which can be a difficult and very time-consuming process.

ARIMA

In 1970, the mathematicians George Box and Gwilym Jenkins published *Time Series: Forecasting and Control*, which described what is now known as the **Box-Jenkins model**. This methodology took the idea of the moving average further with the development of **ARIMA**. As a term, ARIMA is often used interchangeably with Box-Jenkins, although technically, Box-Jenkins refers to a method of parameter optimization for an ARIMA model.

ARIMA is an acronym of three concepts: **Autoregressive (AR)**, **Integrated (I)**, and **Moving Average (MA)**. We already understand the moving average part. **Autoregressive** means that the model uses the dependent relationship between a data point and some number of lagged data points. That is, the model predicts upcoming values based upon previous values. This is similar to predicting that it will be warm tomorrow because it's been warm all week so far.

The **integrated** part means that instead of using any raw data point, the difference between that data point and some previous data point is used. Essentially, this means that we convert a series of values into a series of changes in values. Intuitively, this suggests that tomorrow will be more or less the same temperature as today because the temperature all week hasn't varied too much.

Each of the AR, I, and MA components of an ARIMA model are explicitly specified as a parameter in the model. Traditionally, p is used as the number of lag observations to use, also known as the **lag order**. The number of times that a raw observation is differenced, or the degree of differencing, is known as d, and q represents the size of the moving average window. Thus arises the standard notation for an ARIMA model of *ARIMA(p, d, q)*, where p, d, and q are all non-negative integers.

A problem with ARIMA models is that they do not support seasonality, or data with repeating cycles, such as temperature rising in the day and falling at night or rising in summer and falling in winter. **SARIMA**, or **Seasonal ARIMA**, was developed to overcome this drawback. Similar to the ARIMA notation, the notation for a SARIMA model is *SARIMA(p, d, q)(P, D, Q)m*, with *P* being the seasonal autoregressive order, *D* the seasonal difference order, *Q* the seasonal moving average order, and *m* the number of time steps for a single seasonal period.

You may also come across other variations on ARIMA models, including **VARIMA** (**Vector ARIMA**, for cases with multiple time series as vectors); **FARIMA (Fractional ARIMA)** or **ARFIMA (Fractionally Integrated ARMA)**, both of which include a fractional differencing degree allowing a long memory in the sense that observations far apart in time can have non-negligible dependencies; and **SARIMAX**, a **seasonal ARIMA** model where the *X* stands for exogenous or additional variables added to the model, such as adding a rain forecast to a temperature model.

ARIMA does typically exhibit very good results, but the downside is complexity. Tuning and optimizing ARIMA models is often computationally expensive and successful results can depend upon the skill and experience of the forecaster. It is not a scalable process, but better suited to ad hoc analyses by skilled practitioners.

ARCH/GARCH

When the variance of a dataset is not constant over time, ARIMA models face problems with modeling it. In economics and finance, in particular, this can be common. In a financial time series, large returns tend to be followed by large returns and small returns tend to be followed by small returns. The former is called **high volatility**, and the latter **low volatility**.

Autoregressive Conditional Heteroscedasticity (ARCH) models were developed to solve this problem. **Heteroscedasticity** is a fancy way of saying that the variance or spread of the data is not constant throughout, with the opposite term being **homoscedasticity**. The difference is visualized here:

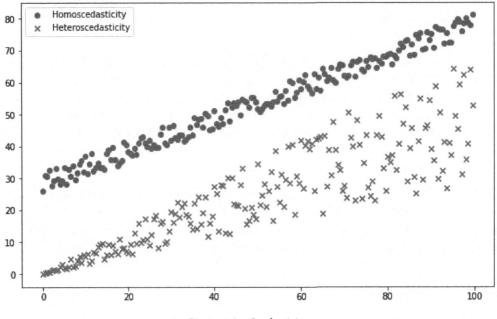

Figure 1.3 – Scedasticity

Robert Engle introduced the first ARCH model in 1982 by describing the **conditional variance** as a function of previous values. For example, there is a lot more uncertainty about daytime electricity usage than there is about nighttime usage. In a model of electricity usage, then, we might assume that the daytime hours have a particular variance, and usage during the night would have a lower variance.

Tim Bollerslev and Stephen Taylor introduced a moving average component to the model in 1986 with their **Generalized ARCH model**, or **GARCH**. In the electricity example, the variance in usage was a function of time of day. But perhaps the swings in volatility don't necessarily occur at specific times of the day, but the swings are themselves random. This is when GARCH is useful.

Both ARCH and GARCH models can handle neither trend nor seasonality though, so often, in practice, an ARIMA model may first be built to extract out the seasonal variation and trend of a time series, and then an ARCH model may be used to model the expected variance.

Neural networks

A relatively recent development in time series forecasting is the use of **Recurrent Neural Networks (RNNs)**. This was made possible with the development of the **Long Short-Term Memory** unit, or **LSTM**, by Sepp Hochreiter and Jürgen Schmidhuber in 1997. Essentially, an LSTM unit allows a neural network to process a sequence of data, such as speech or video, instead of a single data point, such as an image.

A standard RNN is called *recurrent* because it has loops built into it, which is what gives it memory, that is, gives it access to previous information. A basic neural network can be trained to recognize an image of a pedestrian on a street by learning what a pedestrian looks like from previous images, but it cannot be trained to identify that a pedestrian in a video will soon be crossing the street based upon the pedestrian's approach observed in previous frames of the video. It has no knowledge of the sequence of images that leads to the pedestrian stepping out into the road. Short-term memory is what the network needs temporarily to provide context, but that memory degrades quickly.

Early RNNs had a memory problem: it just wasn't very long. In the sentence *airplanes fly in the ...*, a simple RNN may be able to guess the next word will be *sky*. But with *I went to France for vacation last summer. That's why I spent my spring learning to speak ...*, it's not so easy for the RNN to guess that *French* comes next; it understands that the word for a language should come next but has forgotten that the phrase started by mentioning France. An LSTM, though, gives it this necessary context. It gives the network's short-term memory more longevity. In the case of time series data where patterns can reoccur over long time scales, LSTMs can perform very well.

Time series forecasting with LSTMs is still in its infancy when compared to the other forecasting methods discussed here; however, it is showing promise. One strong advantage over other forecasting techniques is the ability of neural networks to capture non-linear relationships. But as with any deep learning problem though, LSTM forecasting requires a great deal of data, computing power, and processing time.

Additionally, there are many decisions to be made regarding the architecture of the model and the hyperparameters to be used, which necessitate a very experienced forecaster. In most practical problems, where budget and deadlines must be considered, an ARIMA model is often the better choice.

Prophet

Prophet was developed internally at Facebook by Sean J. Taylor and Ben Letham in order to overcome two issues often encountered with other forecasting methodologies: the more automatic forecasting tools available tended to be too inflexible and unable to accommodate additional assumptions, and the more robust forecasting tools would require an experienced analyst with specialized data science skills. Facebook was experiencing too much demand for high-quality business forecasts than their analysts were able to provide. In 2017, Facebook released Prophet to the public as open source software.

Prophet was designed to optimally handle business forecasting tasks, which typically feature any of these attributes:

- Time series data captured at the hourly, daily, or weekly level with ideally at least a full year of historical data

- Strong seasonality effects occurring daily, weekly, and/or yearly

- Holidays and other special one-time events that don't necessarily follow the seasonality patterns but occur irregularly

- Missing data and outliers

- Significant trend changes that may occur with the launch of new features or products, for example

- Trends that asymptotically approach an upper or lower bound

Out of the box, Prophet typically produces very high-quality forecasts. But it is also very customizable and approachable by data analysts with no prior expertise in time series data. As you'll see in later chapters, tuning a Prophet model is very intuitive.

Essentially, Prophet is an **additive regression model**. This means that the model is simply the sum of several (optional) components, such as the following:

- A linear or logistic growth trend curve

- An annual seasonality curve

- A weekly seasonality curve

- A daily seasonality curve

- Holidays and other special events

- Additional user-specified seasonality curves, such as hourly or quarterly, for example

To take a concrete example, let's say we are modeling the sales of a small online retail store over four years, from January 1, 2000, through the end of 2003. We observe that the overall trend is constantly increasing over time from **1000** sales per day to around **1800** at the end of the time period. We also see that sales in spring are about **50** units above average and sales in autumn are about **50** units below average. Weekly, sales tend to be lowest on **Tuesday** and increase throughout the week, peaking on **Saturday**. Finally, throughout the hours of the day, sales peak at noon and smoothly fall to their lowest at midnight. This is what those individual curves would look like (note the different *x*-axis scales on each chart):

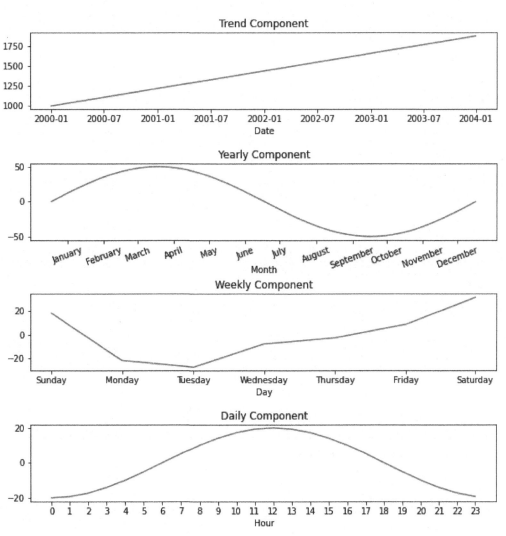

Figure 1.4 – Model components

An additive model would take those four curves and simply add them to each other to arrive at the final model for sales throughout the years. The final curve gets more and more complex as the sub-components are added up:

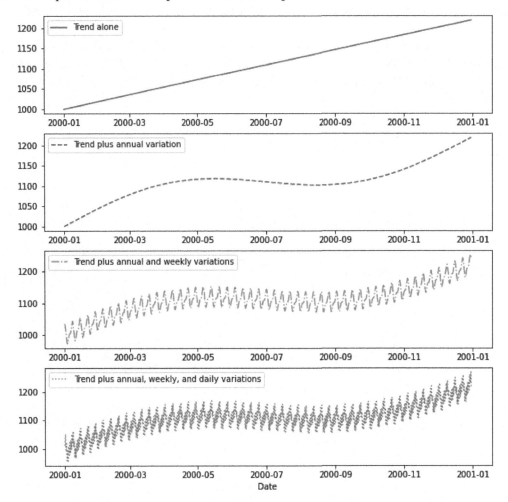

Figure 1.5 – Additive model

This preceding plot displays just the first year to better see the weekly and daily variations, but the full curve extends for 4 years.

Under the hood, Prophet is written in **Stan**, a probabilistic programming language (see the home page at `https://mc-stan.org/` for more information about Stan). This has several advantages. It allows Prophet to optimize the fit process so that it typically completes in under a second. Stan is also compatible with both Python and R, so the Prophet team is able to share the same core fitting procedure between both language implementations. Also, by using Bayesian statistics, Stan allows Prophet to create uncertainty intervals for future predictions to add a data-driven estimate of forecasting risk.

Prophet manages to achieve typical results just as good as the more complicated forecasting techniques but with just a fraction of the effort. It has something for everyone. The beginner can build a highly accurate model in just a few lines of code without necessarily understanding the details of how everything works, while the expert can dig deep into the model, adding more features and tweaking hyperparameters to eke out incrementally better performance.

Summary

With this brief survey of time series, you have learned why time series data can be problematic if not analyzed with specialized techniques. You have followed the developments of mathematicians and statisticians as they have created new techniques to achieve higher forecasting accuracy or more ease of use. You've also learned what motivated the Prophet team to add their own contributions to this legacy and what decisions they made in their approach.

In the next chapter, you'll learn how to get Prophet running on your machine and build your first model. By the end of this book, you'll understand every feature, no matter how small, and have them all in your toolbox to supercharge your own forecasts.

2

Getting Started with Facebook Prophet

Prophet is an open source piece of software, which means that the entirety of the underlying code is freely available to anyone to inspect and modify. This gives Prophet a great deal of power as any user can add features or fix bugs, but it also has its downsides. Many closed source software packages, such as Microsoft Word or Tableau, come packaged in their own independent installation file with a neat graphical user interface to not only walk users through installation but also enable them to interact with the software once it's installed.

Prophet, in contrast, is accessed through either the **Python** or **R** programming languages and depends upon many additional open source libraries. This gives it great flexibility as users can tweak features or even add entirely new ones to suit their specific problem, but it comes with the downside of potentially difficult usability. That's what this book aims to simplify.

In this chapter, we will walk you through the entire installation procedure depending upon which operating system you use, and then together we will build our first forecast by modeling atmospheric carbon dioxide levels over the last few decades.

In full, this chapter will cover the following:

- Installing Prophet
- Building a simple model in Prophet
- Interpreting the forecast DataFrame
- Understanding components plots

Technical requirements

The data files and code for examples in this chapter can be found at `https://github.com/PacktPublishing/Forecasting-Time-Series-Data-with-Facebook-Prophet`. In this chapter, we will walk through the process of installing many of the requirements. So, to begin this chapter, it is only necessary that you have a Windows, macOS, or Linux machine capable of running Anaconda with Python 3.x.

Installing Prophet

Installing Facebook Prophet on your machine is an easy and straightforward process. However, under the hood, Prophet depends upon the **Stan** programming language, and installing **PyStan**, the Python interface for it, is unfortunately not so straightforward because it requires many non-standard compilers.

But don't worry, because there is a really easy way to get Prophet and all dependencies installed, no matter which operating system you use, and that is through Anaconda.

Anaconda is a free distribution of Python that comes bundled with hundreds of additional Python packages that are useful for data science, along with the package management system **conda**. This is in contrast to installing the Python language from its source on `https://www.python.org/`, which will include the default Python package manager, called **pip**.

When `pip` installs a new package, it will install any dependencies without checking whether these dependent Python packages will conflict with others. This can be a particular problem when one package requires a dependency of one version, while another package requires a different version. You may have, for example, a working installation of Google's TensorFlow package, which requires the NumPy package to work with large, multidimensional arrays, and use `pip` to install a new package that specifies a different NumPy version as a dependency.

The different version of NumPy would then overwrite the other version and you may find that TensorFlow suddenly doesn't work as expected, or even at all. In contrast, conda will analyze the current environment and work out on its own how to install a compatible set of dependencies for all installed packages and provide a warning if this cannot be done.

PyStan, and many other Python tools, for that matter, require compilers written in the C language. These types of dependencies are unable to be installed using pip, but Anaconda already includes them. Therefore, it *is strongly recommended to first install Anaconda.*

If you already have a Python environment that you are happy with and do not want to install the full Anaconda distribution, there is a much smaller version available called **Miniconda**, which only includes conda, Python, and a small number of required packages. Although it is technically possible to install Prophet and all dependencies without Anaconda, it can be extremely difficult and the procedure varies a great deal depending on the machine in use, so writing a single guide to cover all scenarios is nearly impossible.

This guide assumes that you will begin with an Anaconda or Miniconda installation, with Python 3 or greater. If you're unsure of whether you want Anaconda or Miniconda, go with Anaconda. Note that the full Anaconda distribution will require about 3 GB of space on your computer due to all of the packages included, so if space is an issue, you should consider Miniconda instead.

> **Important note**
> As of Prophet version 0.6, Python 2 is no longer supported. Be sure that you have Python 3 installed on your machine before proceeding. Installing Anaconda is strongly recommended.

Installation on macOS

If you do not already have Anaconda or Miniconda installed, that should be your first step. Instructions for Anaconda installation can be found in the Anaconda documentation at https://docs.anaconda.com/anaconda/install/mac-os/. If you know that you want Miniconda over Anaconda, start here: https://docs.conda.io/projects/continuumio-conda/en/latest/user-guide/install/macos.html. Use all of the defaults for installation in either case.

With Anaconda or Miniconda installed, installing Prophet can be achieved using `conda`. Simply run the following two commands in the terminal to first install `gcc`, a collection of compilers that PyStan requires, and then install Prophet itself, which will automatically also install PyStan:

```
conda install gcc
conda install -c conda-forge fbprophet
```

And after that, you should be able to get started! You can skip ahead to the next section where we see how to build your first model.

Installation on Windows

As with macOS, the first step is to ensure that Anaconda or Miniconda is installed. Anaconda installation instructions can be found at `https://docs.anaconda.com/anaconda/install/windows/`, and those for Miniconda are available here: `https://docs.conda.io/projects/continuumio-conda/en/latest/user-guide/install/windows.html`.

On Windows, you must check the box to register Anaconda as the default Python. This is required to get PyStan installed correctly. You may see a different version of Python, such as Python 3.8, than shown here:

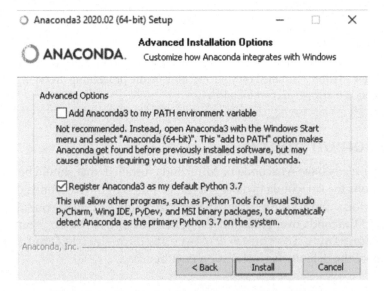

Figure 2.1 – Registering Anaconda as the default Python

Once Anaconda or Miniconda is installed, you'll have access to the **conda package manager**, which greatly simplifies Prophet's installation on Windows by getting around many issues with PyStan installation. First, install `gcc`, which is a collection of compilers that PyStan requires, and then install Prophet itself, which will automatically also install PyStan, by running the following two commands in your Command Prompt:

```
conda install gcc
conda install -c conda-forge fbprophet
```

That second command includes additional syntax to instruct `conda` to look at the `conda-forge` channel for the Facebook Prophet files. `conda-forge` is a community effort that allows developers to provide their software as a `conda` package. Prophet is not included in the default Anaconda distribution, but with the `conda-forge` channel, and the Facebook team can provide access directly through conda.

That should leave you with Prophet successfully installed!

Installation on Linux

Installing Anaconda on Linux requires just a few additional steps compared with macOS or Windows, but they should not pose any problems. Full instructions can be found in Anaconda's documentation at `https://docs.anaconda.com/anaconda/ install/linux/`. Instructions for Miniconda are available at `https://docs. conda.io/projects/continuumio-conda/en/latest/user-guide/ install/linux.html`.

Because Linux is offered by various distributions, it is not possible to write a fully comprehensive guide for Prophet installation. However, if you are already using Linux, it is a fair assumption that you are also well versed in its intricacies.

Just make sure that you have the `gcc`, `g++`, and `build-essential` compilers installed and the `python-dev` and `python3-dev` Python development tools. If your Linux distribution is a Red Hat system, install `gcc64` and `gcc64-c++`. After that, use `conda` to install Prophet:

```
conda install -c conda-forge fbprophet
```

If everything went well, you should be ready to go now! Let's test it out by building your first model.

Building a simple model in Prophet

The longest record of direct measurements of CO_2 in the atmosphere was started in March 1958 by Charles David Keeling of the Scripps Institution of Oceanography. Keeling was based in La Jolla, California, but had received permission from the **National Oceanic and Atmospheric Administration (NOAA)** to use their facility located two miles above sea level on the northern slope of Mauna Loa, a volcano on the island of Hawaii, to collect carbon dioxide samples. At that elevation, Keeling's measurements would be unaffected by local releases of CO_2 such as from nearby factories.

In 1961, Keeling published the data he had collected thus far, establishing that there was strong seasonal variation in CO_2 levels and that they were rising steadily, a trend that later became known as the **Keeling Curve**. By May 1974, the NOAA had begun their own parallel measurements and have continued since then. The Keeling Curve graph is as follows:

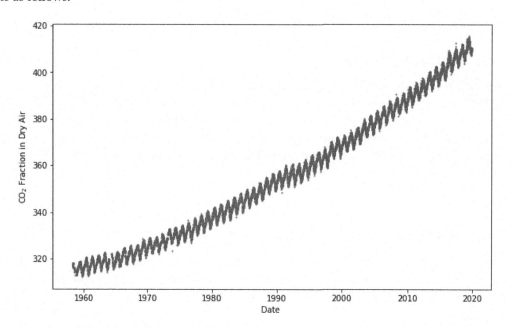

Figure 2.2 – The Keeling Curve, showing the concentration of carbon dioxide in the atmosphere

With its seasonality and increasing trend, this curve is a good candidate to try out Prophet. This dataset contains over 19,000 daily observations across 53 years. The unit of measurement for CO_2 is *PPM*, or *parts per million*, a measure of CO_2 molecules per million molecules of air.

To begin our model, we need to import the necessary libraries, `pandas` and `Matplotlib`, and import the Prophet class from the `fbprophet` package:

```
import pandas as pd
import matplotlib.pyplot as plt
from fbprophet import Prophet
```

As input, Prophet always requires a pandas DataFrame with two columns:

- `ds`, for datestamp, should be a `datestamp` or `timestamp` column in a format expected by pandas.

- `y`, a numeric column containing the measurement we wish to forecast.

Here, we use pandas to import the data, in this case a `csv` file, and then load it into a DataFrame. Note that we also convert the `ds` column to a pandas datetime format, to ensure that pandas is correctly identifying it as dates and not simply loading it as an alphanumeric string:

```
df = pd.read_csv('co2-ppm-daily_csv.csv')
df['date'] = pd.to_datetime(df['date'])
df.columns = ['ds', 'y']
```

If you're familiar with the scikit-learn (`sklearn`) package, you'll feel right at home in Prophet because it was designed to operate in a similar way. Prophet follows the sklearn paradigm of first creating an instance of the model class before calling the `fit` and `predict` methods:

```
model = Prophet()
model.fit(df)
```

In that single `fit` command, Prophet analyzed the data and isolated both the seasonality and trend without requiring us to specify any additional parameters. It has not yet made any future forecast, though. To do that, we need to first make a DataFrame of future dates and then call the `predict` method. The `make_future_dataframe` method requires us to specify the number of days we intend to forecast out. In this case, we will choose 10 years, or `365` days, times `10`:

```
future = model.make_future_dataframe(periods=365 * 10)
forecast = model.predict(future)
```

At this point, the `forecast` DataFrame contains Prophet's prediction for CO_2 concentrations going 10 years into the future. We will explore that DataFrame in a moment, but first let's plot the data using Prophet's `plot` functionality. The `plot` method is built upon Matplotlib; it requires a DataFrame output from the `predict` method (our `forecast` DataFrame in this example).

We're labeling the axes with the optional `xlabel` and `ylabel` arguments, but just sticking with the default for the optional `figsize` argument. Note that I am also adding a title using raw Matplotlib syntax; because the Prophet plot is built upon Matplotlib, anything you can do to a Matplotlib figure can be performed here as well. Also, don't be confused by the odd `ylabel` text with the dollar signs; that just tells Matplotlib to use its own TeX-like engine to make the subscript in CO_2:

```
fig = model.plot(forecast, xlabel='Date',
                 ylabel=r'CO$_2$ PPM')
plt.title('Daily Carbon Dioxide Levels Measured at Mauna Loa')
plt.show()
```

The graph is as follows:

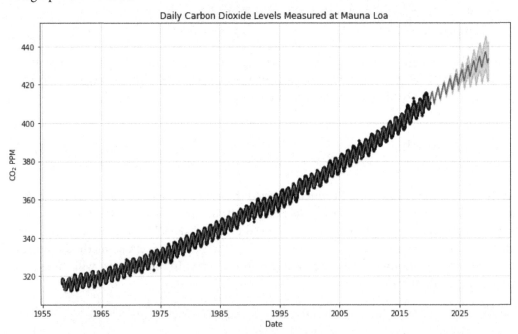

Figure 2.3 – Prophet forecast

And that's it! In those 12 lines of code, we have arrived at our 10-year forecast.

Interpreting the forecast DataFrame

Now, let's take a look at that `forecast` DataFrame by displaying the first three rows (I've transposed it here, in order to better see the column names on the page) and learn how these values were used in the preceding chart:

```
forecast.head(3).T
```

After running that command, you should see the following table print out:

	0	1	2
ds	1958-03-30 00:00:00	1958-03-31 00:00:00	1958-04-02 00:00:00
trend	314.876	314.879	314.883
yhat_lower	316.034	316.059	316.172
yhat_upper	317.776	317.767	317.853
trend_lower	314.876	314.879	314.883
trend_upper	314.876	314.879	314.883
additive_terms	1.98563	2.01564	2.11873
additive_terms_lower	1.98563	2.01564	2.11873
additive_terms_upper	1.98563	2.01564	2.11873
weekly	0.00324593	-0.0107885	0.00339251
weekly_lower	0.00324593	-0.0107885	0.00339251
weekly_upper	0.00324593	-0.0107885	0.00339251
yearly	1.98239	2.02643	2.11534
yearly_lower	1.98239	2.02643	2.11534
yearly_upper	1.98239	2.02643	2.11534
multiplicative_terms	0	0	0
multiplicative_terms_lower	0	0	0
multiplicative_terms_upper	0	0	0
yhat	316.862	316.894	317.002

Figure 2.4 – The forecast DataFrame

The following is a description of each of the columns in the `forecast` DataFrame:

- `'ds'`: Datestamp or timestamp that values in that row pertain to
- `'trend'`: Value of the trend component alone
- `'yhat_lower'`: Lower bound of the uncertainty interval around the final prediction
- `'yhat_upper'`: Upper bound of the uncertainty interval around the final prediction
- `'trend_lower'`: Lower bound of the uncertainty interval around the trend component
- `'trend_upper'`: Upper bound of the uncertainty interval around the trend component
- `'additive_terms'`: Combined value of all the additive seasonalities
- `'additive_terms_lower'`: Lower bound of the uncertainty interval around the additive seasonalities
- `'additive_terms_upper'`: Upper bound of the uncertainty interval around the additive seasonalities
- `'weekly'`: Value of the weekly seasonality component
- `'weekly_lower'`: Lower bound of the uncertainty interval around the weekly component
- `'weekly_upper'`: Upper bound of the uncertainty interval around the weekly component
- `'yearly'`: Value of the yearly seasonality component
- `'yearly_lower'`: Lower bound of the uncertainty interval around the yearly component
- `'yearly_upper'`: Upper bound of the uncertainty interval around the yearly component
- `'multiplicative_terms'`: Combined value of all the multiplicative seasonalities
- `'multiplicative_terms_lower'`: Lower bound of the uncertainty interval around the multiplicative seasonalities

- `'multiplicative_terms_upper'`: Upper bound of the uncertainty interval around the multiplicative seasonalities

- `'yhat'`: Final predicted value; a combination of `'trend'`, `'multiplicative_terms'`, and `'additive_terms'`

If the data contains a daily seasonality, then columns for `'daily'`, `'daily_upper'`, and `'daily_lower'` will also be included, following the pattern established with the `'weekly'` and `'yearly'` columns. Later chapters will include discussion and examples of both the additive/multiplicative seasonalities and of the uncertainty intervals.

> **Tip**
> *yhat* is pronounced as *why hat*. It comes from the statistical notation where the variable $\hat{y}$ represents a predicted value of the variable y. In general, placing a hat, or caret, over a true parameter denotes an estimator of it.

In *Figure 2.3*, the black dots represent the actual recorded y values we fit on (those in the `df['y']` column), whereas the solid line represents the calculated `yhat` values (the `forecast['yhat']` column). Note that the solid line extends beyond the range of the black dots where we have forecasted into the future. The lighter shading notable around the solid line in the forecasted region represents the uncertainty interval, bound by `forecast['yhat_lower']` and `forecast['yhat_upper']`.

Now let's break down that forecast into its components.

Understanding components plots

In *Chapter 1*, The *History and Development of Time Series Forecasting*, Prophet was introduced as an additive regression model. *Figures 1.4 and 1.5* showed how individual component curves for the trend and the different seasonalities are added together to create a more complex curve. The Prophet algorithm essentially does this in reverse; it takes a complex curve and decomposes it into its constituent parts. The first step toward greater control of a Prophet forecast is to understand these components so that they can be manipulated individually. Prophet provides a `plot_components` method to visualize these.

Continuing on with our progress on the Mauna Loa model, plotting the components is as simple as running these commands:

```
fig2 = model.plot_components(forecast)
plt.show()
```

As you can see in the output plot, Prophet has isolated three components in this dataset: **trend**, **weekly seasonality**, and **yearly seasonality**:

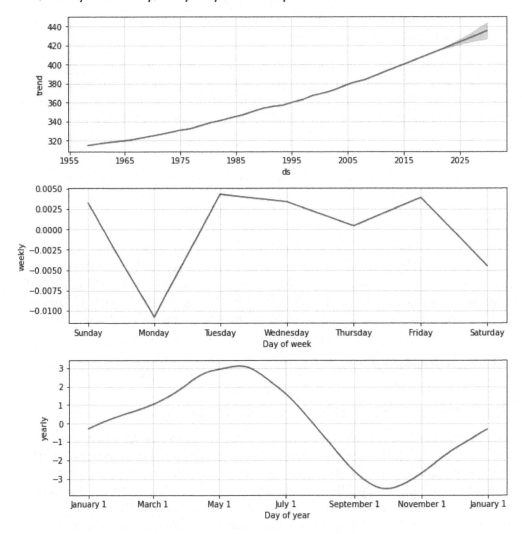

Figure 2.5 – Mauna Loa components plot

The **trend** constantly increases but seems to have a steepening slope as time progresses—an acceleration of CO_2 concentration in the atmosphere. The trend line also shows slim uncertainty intervals in the forecasted year. From this curve, we learn that atmospheric CO_2 concentrations were about 320 ppm in 1965. This grew to about 400 by 2015 and we expect about 430 PPM by 2030. However, these exact numbers will vary depending upon the day of the week and the time of year, due to the existence of the seasonality effects.

The **weekly seasonality** shows that by days of the week, values will vary by about 0.01 PPM—an insignificant amount and most likely due purely to noise and random chance. Indeed, intuition tells us that carbon dioxide levels (when measured far enough away from human activity, as they are on the high slopes of Mauna Loa) do not care much what day of the week it is and are unaffected by it.

We will learn in *Chapter 4, Seasonality*, how to instruct Prophet not to fit a weekly seasonality, as is prudent in this case. In *Chapter 10, Uncertainty Intervals*, we will learn how to plot uncertainty for seasonality and ensure that a seasonality such as this can be ignored.

Now, looking at the **yearly seasonality** reveals that carbon dioxide rises throughout the winter and peaks in May or so, while falling in the summer with a trough in October. Measurements of carbon dioxide can be 3 PPM above or 3 PPM below what the trend alone would predict, based upon the time of year. If you refer back to the original data, plotted in *Figure 2.2*, you will be reminded that there was a very obvious cyclical nature to the curve, captured with this yearly seasonality.

As simple as that model was, that is often all you need to make very accurate forecasts with Prophet! We used no additional parameters than the defaults and yet achieved very good results.

Summary

Hopefully, you experienced no issues installing Prophet on your machine at the beginning of this chapter. The potential challenge of getting the Stan dependency installed is greatly eased by using the Anaconda distribution of Python. After installation, we looked at the carbon dioxide levels measured in the atmosphere two miles above the Pacific Ocean, at Mauna Loa in Hawaii. We built our first Prophet model and, in just 12 lines of code, were able to forecast the next 10 years of carbon dioxide levels.

After that, we inspected the `forecast` DataFrame and saw the rich results that Prophet outputs. Finally, we plotted the components of the forecast - the trend, yearly seasonality, and weekly seasonality, to better understand the data's behavior.

There is a lot more to Prophet than just this simple example, though. The remainder of this book will be spent demonstrating all of the parameters and additional features available that allow you to have greater control over your forecasts. Next, we'll take a look at non-daily data to see what precautions and adjustments need to be taken, thereby preparing us to handle datasets with different time granularities.

Section 2: Seasonality, Tuning, and Advanced Features

This section will teach you about the advanced features of Prophet. Every adjustable parameter will be explored with examples and a discussion of why and how to modify them. Each chapter builds on the previous chapters to add more and more complexity and power to the forecasting models. By the end of the section, you will be able to build models that harness the full capability of Prophet's forecasting toolset.

This section comprises the following chapters:

3
Non-Daily Data

When Prophet was first released, it assumed all data would be on a daily scale, with one row of data per day. It has since grown to handle many different granularities of data, but because of its historical conventions, there are few things to be cautious of when working with non-daily data.

In this chapter, you will look at monthly data (and in fact, any data that is measured in timeframes greater than a day) and see how to change the frequency of predictions to avoid unexpected results. You will also look at hourly data and observe an additional component in the components plot. Finally, you will learn how to handle data that has regular gaps along the time axis.

This chapter will cover the following:

- Using monthly data
- Using sub-daily data
- Using data with regular gaps

Technical requirements

The data files and code for examples in this chapter can be found at https://github.com/PacktPublishing/Forecasting-Time-Series-Data-with-Facebook-Prophet.

Please refer to the *Preface* of this book for the technical requirements necessary to run the code examples.

Using monthly data

In *Chapter 2*, *Getting Started with Facebook Prophet*, we built our first Prophet model using the Mauna Loa dataset. The data was reported every day, which is what Prophet by default will expect and is therefore why we did not need to change any of Prophet's default parameters. In this next example, though, let's take a look at a new set of data that is not reported every day, the Air Passengers dataset, to see how Prophet handles this difference in data granularity.

This is a classic time series dataset spanning 1949 through 1960. It counts the number of passengers on commercial airlines each month during that period of explosive growth in the industry. The Air Passengers dataset, in contrast to the Mauna Loa dataset, has one observation per month. What happens if we attempt to predict future dates?

Let's create a model and plot the forecast to see what happens. We begin as we did with the Mauna Loa example, by importing the necessary libraries and loading our data into a properly formatted DataFrame:

```
import pandas as pd
import matplotlib.pyplot as plt
from fbprophet import Prophet

df = pd.read_csv('AirPassengers.csv')
df['Month'] = pd.to_datetime(df['Month'])
df.columns = ['ds', 'y']
```

Before building our model, let's just take a look at the first few rows to ensure that our DataFrame looks as expected:

```
df.head()
```

You should now see this output:

	ds	y
0	1949-01-01	112
1	1949-02-01	118
2	1949-03-01	132
3	1949-04-01	129
4	1949-05-01	121

Figure 3.1 – The Air Passengers DataFrame

The data is reported on a monthly basis, with one measurement for each month. Passenger numbers are reported per thousand, which means that the first row indicates that 112,000 commercial passengers took to the skies during the month beginning January 1, 1949.

Just as we did with Mauna Loa in the previous chapter, we will next instantiate our model and fit it. With this Air Passengers dataset, we will set seasonality_mode to 'multiplicative', but don't concern yourself with this for now—we'll cover it in *Chapter 4, Seasonality*. Next, we send our data to the fit method and then make a future DataFrame. Let's forecast 5 years. Finally, we will use predict with the future and then plot the forecast to see how we did:

```
model = Prophet(seasonality_mode='multiplicative')
model.fit(df)
future = model.make_future_dataframe(periods=365 * 5)
forecast = model.predict(future)
fig = model.plot(forecast)
plt.show()
```

As you can see, we created our `future` DataFrame with 5 years of daily data, but we provided Prophet with monthly data. Prophet is able to apply its seasonality calculations appropriately on the first day of each month, where it has good training data. For the remaining days, though, it doesn't quite know what to do and overfits its seasonality curve in wild and unpredictable ways, as can be seen in the following graph:

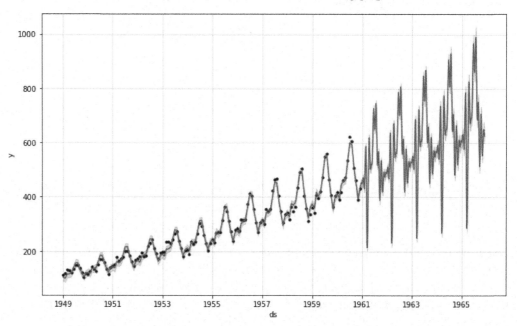

Figure 3.2 – Future forecast with daily frequency

We can fix this by instructing Prophet to only forecast on a monthly scale, to match the monthly data it is trained on. We need to specify a frequency in the `make_future_dataframe` method, and we do this by passing the `freq` argument. We must also update `periods` because although we are still forecasting 5 years into the future, we only want 12 entries per year, one for each month:

```
model = Prophet(seasonality_mode='multiplicative')
model.fit(df)
future = model.make_future_dataframe(periods=12 * 5,
                                     freq='MS')
forecast = model.predict(future)
fig = model.plot(forecast)
plt.show()
```

The `freq` argument accepts anything that pandas identifies as a frequency string. In this case, we used `'MS'`, for month start. Here is the output of that code block, the plotted forecast once Prophet is instructed to predict only on the first day of each month:

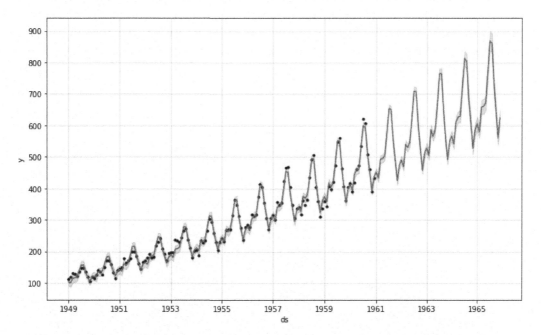

Figure 3.3 – Future forecast with monthly frequency

That's much better, exactly what we might expect the forecast to look like. By feeding the `freq` argument to the `make_future_dataframe` method, we do not make the mistake of asking Prophet to forecast dates for which it has no training knowledge. By default, the frequency is set to `'D'`, for daily, and our periods would be the number of days we want to forecast. Whenever changing the frequency to some other setting, be sure to set your periods to be on the same scale.

Now let's see what changes when we use data on the sub-daily scale. To do that, I'll introduce a new dataset: Divvy.

Using sub-daily data

In this section, we will be using data from the **Divvy bike share program** in Chicago, Illinois. The data contains the number of bicycle rides taken each hour from the beginning of 2014 through the end of 2018 and exhibits a general increasing trend along with very strong yearly seasonality. Because it is hourly data and there are very few rides overnight (sometimes zero per hour), the data does show a density of measurements at the low end:

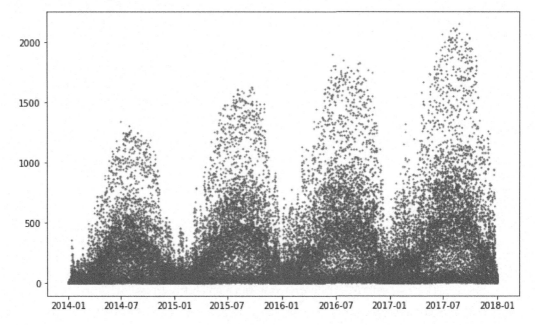

Figure 3.4 – Divvy number of rides per hour

Using **sub-daily data** such as this is much the same as using **super-daily data**, as we did with the `Air Passengers` data previously. You as the analyst need to use the `freq` argument and adjust the periods in the `make_future_dataframe` method, and Prophet will do the rest. If Prophet sees at least two days of data and the spacing between data is less than one day, it will fit a daily seasonality.

Let's see this by making a simple forecast. We already imported the necessary libraries in the previous example, so let's continue by loading the new data and adding it to our DataFrame:

```
data = pd.read_csv('divvy_hourly.csv')
df = pd.DataFrame({'ds': pd.to_datetime(data['date']),
                   'y': data['rides']})
```

Next, we continue as we did in the previous example by instantiating our model (again, using seasonality_mode='multiplicative', and again, not worrying about it for now) before fitting our model. When we create the future DataFrame, we again need to set a frequency but this time we will use 'h', for hourly.

Now that our frequency is hourly, we need to adjust our period to match, so we multiply the 365-day forecast we want by 24 hours per day:

```
model = Prophet(seasonality_mode='multiplicative')
model.fit(df)
future = model.make_future_dataframe(periods=365 * 24,
                                     freq='h')
```

Finally, we will predict our future DataFrame. With our forecast complete, we will plot it in the first plot function and then the components in the second plot function:

```
forecast = model.predict(future)
fig = model.plot(forecast)
plt.show()
fig2 = model.plot_components(forecast)
plt.show()
```

The first of those two plots is the forecast that follows:

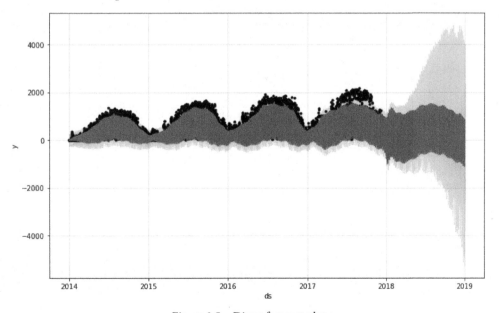

Figure 3.5 – Divvy forecast plot

The forecast includes a rather large amount of uncertainty. To understand why, we need to look at the components plot:

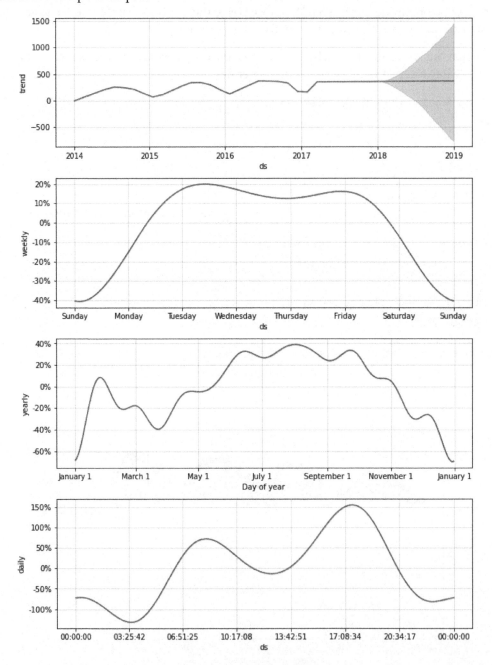

Figure 3.6 – Divvy components plot

There are a few things to note about this series of plots. Starting from the upper-most plot, the **trend** plot, we can see that it still exhibits annual periodicity. Why wasn't this captured in the **yearly seasonality** plot? Unfortunately, this data contains some very complex seasonalities that Prophet is unable to fully model.

In particular, the **daily** seasonality itself is seasonal within the year. It's seasonality within seasonality. The daily seasonality rises in the day and falls in the night, but the amount of the increase is dependent upon the time of year, and Prophet is not built to capture this type of seasonality. This is what causes so much forecast uncertainty. In later chapters, we will learn a few techniques to control this.

Next, we look at the **weekly** seasonality plot. In contrast to the Mauna Loa example in *Chapter 2, Getting Started with Facebook Prophet*, this plot displays a single curved line. The Mauna Loa plot featured several straight-line segments. Also, the plot goes from Sunday to Sunday, whereas the Mauna Loa plot went from Sunday to Saturday. Both of these changes are to reflect the more continuous nature of hourly data.

When we only had daily data, as we did with Mauna Loa, the weekly seasonality only needed to show the effect of each day (although, under the hood, it still is a continuous model). But now that we have hourly data, it is important to see the continuous effect. We are seeing 12:00:00 am on Sunday through 11:59:59 pm on Saturday, which is 1 second shy of 8 days. The Mauna Loa plot in essence showed the daily effect at a single moment each day, exactly 7 days, hence the difference between the two plots.

Now take a look at the **yearly** seasonality. It's quite *wavy*. Just take note of that for now. We'll talk about it in *Chapter 4, Seasonality*, when we learn about **Fourier order**.

Finally, the **daily** seasonality plot. This is new and only appears when Prophet models sub-daily data. It's quite revealing with this dataset, though. It seems that riders in the Divvy network ride a lot around 8am, possibly commuting to work. There is an even larger spike just after 5pm, possibly riders returning home. And finally, there's a small hump just after midnight. These must be the night-owls, who spent the evening out with friends and are returning home to bed.

I also want to mention one more thing about the forecast: the model predicts some negative values, although it's impossible for Divvy to have a negative number of rides taken during any given hour. The Prophet developers are actively working on this issue and will release a solution in a future update.

In the last two sections, you learned that super-daily data and sub-daily data pose no difficult issues to overcome; we can simply adjust the frequency future predictions. But now suppose that Divvy had only been collecting data from 8am until 6pm each day. The last topic to cover in this chapter is how to handle data with regular gaps.

Using data with regular gaps

Throughout your career, you may encounter datasets with regular gaps in reporting, particularly when the data was collected by humans who have working hours, personal hours, and sleeping hours. It simply may not be possible to collect measurements with perfect periodicity.

As you will see when we look at outliers in a later chapter, Prophet is robust in handling missing values. However, when that missing data occurs at regular intervals, Prophet will have no training data at all during those gaps to make estimations with. The seasonality will be constrained during periods where data exists but unconstrained during the gaps, and Prophet's predictions can see much larger fluctuations than the actual data displayed. Let's see this in action.

Suppose that Divvy's data had only been collected between the hours of 8am and 6pm each day. We can simulate this by removing data outside these hours from our DataFrame:

```
df = df[(df['ds'].dt.hour >= 8) & \
        (df['ds'].dt.hour < 18)]
```

Now compare the following plot of this new DataFrame with the full dataset, which we saw in *Figure 3.3*:

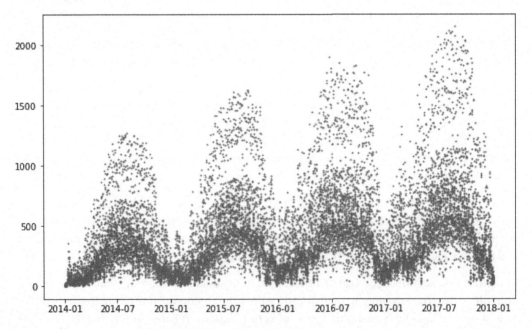

Figure 3.7 – Divvy rides per hour between 8am and 6pm

This plot is much sparser than *Figure 3.3*, being particularly low for the y-axis values. We lost all overnight data, when ridership is down. Each day only has 10 data points now, one for each hour between 8am and 6pm. Now, let's build a forecast model exactly as we did in the previous section, making our `future` DataFrame with one year of hourly frequency, but taking no extra precautions:

```
model = Prophet(seasonality_mode='multiplicative')
model.fit(df)
future = model.make_future_dataframe(periods=365 * 24,
                                     freq='h')
forecast = model.predict(future)
fig = model.plot(forecast)
plt.show()
```

The plotted forecast shows much wider daily fluctuations in the future period than the historical training data:

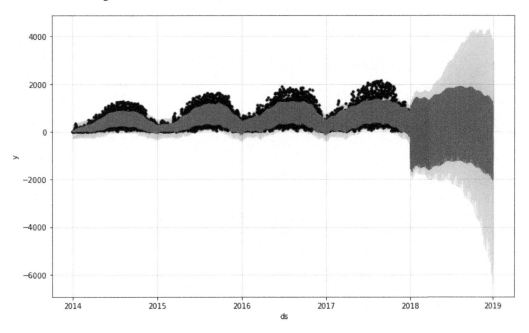

Figure 3.8 – Divvy forecast with regular gaps

What we are seeing there are unconstrained estimates in the future period causing wide fluctuations in predictions. This is the same effect that we observed with the `Air Passengers` data, when we predicted daily forecasts with monthly data. We can zoom in on just 3 days in August 2018 to see more clearly what's going on by replotting and using Matplotlib to constrain the limits of the x and y axes:

```
fig = model.plot(forecast)
plt.xlim(pd.to_datetime(['2018-08-01', '2018-08-04']))
plt.ylim(-2000, 4000)
plt.show()
```

Whereas the forecast plot from before showed 5 years of predictions, this plot shows just 3 days, so you can fully see what's going on:

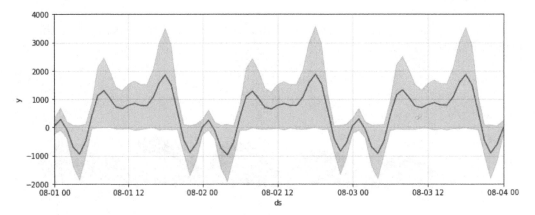

Figure 3.9 – Divvy forecast over 3 days

In the previous section, when we looked at *Figure 3.5*, we noted that the daily seasonality component showed ridership picking up before 8am and hitting a local peak right at 8am. There was a slump at midday and then a large peak right after 6pm. We are seeing the same thing in *Figure 3.8*, except that Prophet is making wild predictions before 8am and after 6pm, where it has no training data. This area is unconstrained and could follow almost any pattern as long as the equations work out for the midday period where data exists.

The solution to this problem is to simply modify the `future` DataFrame to exclude those times where our training data had regular gaps. We don't even need to instantiate a new model or refit; we can just reuse our previous work. So, continuing on, we create a new `future2` DataFrame, remove those times earlier than 8am and later than 6pm, and then predict our forecast and plot the results:

```
future2 = future[(future['ds'].dt.hour >= 8) &
                 (future['ds'].dt.hour < 18)]
forecast2 = model.predict(future2)
fig = model.plot(forecast2)
plt.show()
```

Now we see a good forecast:

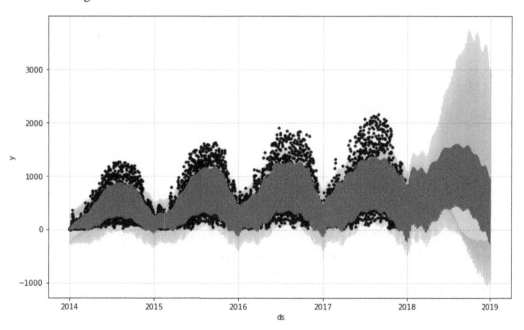

Figure 3.10 – Divvy with regular gaps fixed

The daily fluctuations in the predicted future are of the same magnitude as our historical training data. Contrast that with *Figure 3.7*, where the future period showed a much wider range of predictions. Let's again plot those same 3 days in August to compare with *Figure 3.8*:

```
fig = model.plot(forecast2, figsize=(10, 4))
plt.xlim(pd.to_datetime(['2018-08-01', '2018-08-04']))
plt.ylim(-2000, 4000)
plt.show()
```

We see the same curve as before for the hours between 8am and 6pm, but this time Prophet simply connects them with a straight line. There is, in fact, no data in our `forecast` DataFrame for these time periods; Prophet simply ignores them:

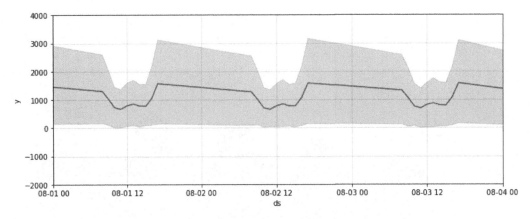

Figure 3.11 – Divvy 3-day forecast with regular gaps fixed

Prophet is a continuous-time model, so although the `forecast` DataFrame ignores those excluded times, the equations that underpin the model are defined continuously. We can observe this by plotting the daily seasonality with the `plot_seasonality` function. This function is contained within Prophet's `plot` package, so we need to import it first. It takes two required arguments, the model and a string identifying the seasonality to plot, and we are also passing an optional argument to change the figure size:

```
from fbprophet.plot import plot_seasonality
plot_seasonality(model, 'daily', figsize=(10, 3))
plt.show()
```

Remember that we did not create a new model to solve the regular gap problem; we only removed those times from our `forecast` DataFrame the second time around. This means that with only one model in these two examples, of course the components are the same. The daily seasonality we plotted is the same for both versions:

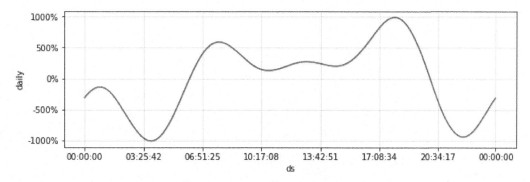

Figure 3.12 – Divvy daily seasonality

As you can see, the period from 8am until 6pm matches both *Figure 3.8* and *Figure 3.10*, even though those two plots showed wildly different results overnight. As we have no training or future data for times outside that range, those times on the daily seasonality plot can be ignored. They are merely mathematical artifacts of the equations that created the midday curve.

Summary

In this chapter, you took the lessons learned from the basic `Mauna Loa` model you built in *Chapter 2, Getting Started with Facebook Prophet*, and learned what changes you need to make when the period of your data is not daily. Specifically, you used the `Air Passengers` dataset to model monthly data and used the `freq` argument when making your `future` DataFrame in order to hold back Prophet from predicting daily.

Then, you used the hourly data from Divvy's bike share program to set the future frequency to hourly so that Prophet would increase the granularity of its prediction timescale. Finally, you simulated periodic missing data in the Divvy dataset and learned a different way to match the `future` DataFrame's schedule to that of the training data, in order to prevent Prophet from making unconstrained predictions.

Now that you know how to handle the different datasets you will encounter in this book, you're ready for the next topic! In the next chapter, you will learn all about seasonality. Seasonality is at the heart of Prophet's power and it's a big topic, so prepare yourself!

4
Seasonality

One quality that sets time series apart from other datasets is that very often—but not always—the data has a certain rhythm to it. That rhythm may be yearly, possibly due to the Earth's rotation around the Sun, or daily, if rooted in the Earth's rotation around its axis. The tidal cycle follows the Moon's rotation around the Earth.

Traffic congestion follows the human activity cycle throughout the day and the five-day workweek followed by the two-day weekend; financial activity follows the quarterly business cycle. Your own body follows cycles due to your heartbeat, breathing rate, and circadian rhythm. On the very small physical and very short temporal scales, the vibration of atoms is a cause of periodicity in data. Prophet calls these cycles **seasonalities**.

In this chapter, you will learn about all the different types of seasonalities Prophet fits by default, how to add new ones, and how to control them. In particular, we will cover the following:

- Understanding additive versus multiplicative seasonality
- Controlling seasonality with Fourier order
- Adding custom seasonalities
- Adding conditional seasonalities
- Regularizing seasonality

Technical requirements

The data files and code for examples in this chapter can be found at
`https://github.com/PacktPublishing/Forecasting-Time-Series-Data-with-Facebook-Prophet`.

Understanding additive versus multiplicative seasonality

In our Mauna Loa example in *Chapter 2, Getting Started with Facebook Prophet*, the yearly seasonality was constant at all values along the trend line. We added the values predicted by the seasonality curve to the values predicted by the trend curve to arrive at our forecast. There is an alternative mode of seasonality though, where we would multiply the trend curve by the seasonality. Take a look at this figure:

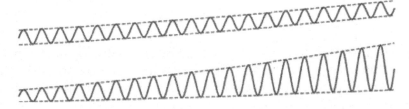

Figure 4.1 – Additive versus multiplicative seasonality

The upper curve demonstrates additive seasonality—the dashed lines that trace the bounds of the seasonality are parallel because the magnitude of seasonality does not change, only the trend does. In the lower curve though, these two dashed lines are not parallel. Where the trend is low, the spread caused by seasonality is low; but where the trend is high, the spread caused by seasonality is high. This can be modeled with multiplicative seasonality.

Let's look at a concrete example using the Air Passengers dataset introduced in the previous chapter. This data records the number of commercial airline passengers per month from 1949 to 1960. We will first model it using Prophet's default `seasonality_mode`, the additive mode that we used with the Mauna Loa example, and then contrast it with the multiplicative mode.

We begin just as we did in the previous chapter, by importing the necessary libraries and loading the data in a DataFrame:

```
import pandas as pd
import matplotlib.pyplot as plt
from fbprophet import Prophet

df = pd.read_csv('AirPassengers.csv')
df ['Month'] = pd.to_datetime(df['Month'])
df.columns = ['ds', 'y']
```

Let's continue building our model. I am calling this one model_a to indicate that it is our additive model, and I'll call the next model model_m, for multiplicative:

```
model_a = Prophet(seasonality_mode='additive',
                  yearly_seasonality=4)
model_a.fit(df)
forecast_a = model_a.predict()
fig_a = model_a.plot(forecast_a)
plt.show()
```

When we instantiated the Prophet object, we explicitly declared seasonality_mode to be 'additive' for clarity's sake. By default, if no seasonality_mode is stated, then Prophet will automatically select 'additive'. Also note that we set yearly_seasonality=4. That merely sets the **Fourier order** for the curve, but don't worry about this for now because we'll go over it in the next section.

After creating the Prophet model, we fit and predicted it just as before in the Mauna Loa example, and then plotted the forecast. Note that in this example though, we never created a future DataFrame—if no future DataFrame is sent to the predict method, it simply creates predicted values for the historical data it received in the fit method but no future predicted values. As we are only interested in seeing how Prophet has handled the seasonality, we don't need a future forecast.

Here is the figure we just created:

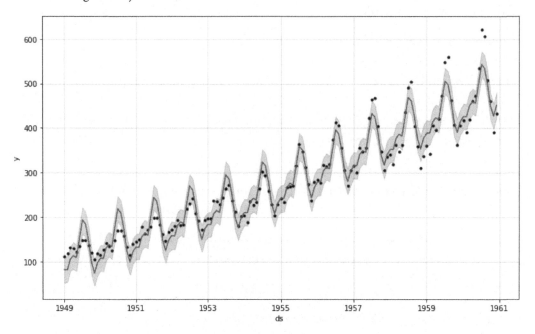

Figure 4.2 – Air passengers with additive seasonality

As you can see, early in the data, in **1949**, **1951**, and **1952**, Prophet's predicted values (the solid line) have large seasonal swings that are more extreme than the data (the dots) indicates. Later in the series, in **1958**, **1959**, and **1960**, Prophet's predicted seasonality is less extreme than the data indicates. The seasonal spread of the data is increasing, but we have predicted it to be constant. That's the mistake of choosing additive seasonality when multiplicative is required. Let's run the model again, but this time we will use multiplicative seasonality:

```
model_m = Prophet(seasonality_mode='multiplicative',
                  yearly_seasonality=4)
model_m.fit(df)
forecast_m = model_m.predict()
fig_m = model_m.plot(forecast_m)
plt.show()
```

We do everything the same as the previous example, except this time we set
`seasonality_mode='multiplicative'`. We see this change reflected
in the figure we produce:

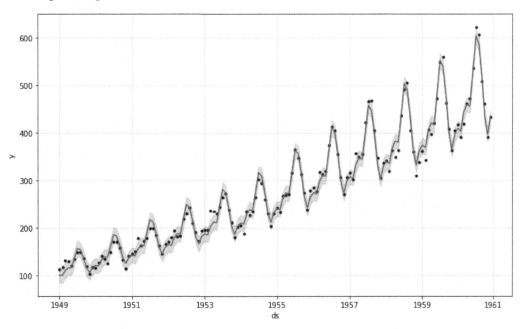

Figure 4.3 – Air passengers with multiplicative seasonality

That's a much better fit! Now, Prophet is matching the growth of the seasonality swings
along with the growth of the overall trend. Also, compare the error estimates between
Figure 4.2 and *Figure 4.3* (the light shaded area surrounding the solid line). Prophet shows
wider uncertainty intervals when it attempts to fit additive seasonality to a series of data
containing multiplicative seasonality. Prophet knows that it does not have a good fit in the
former model and is less certain about its predictions.

There's one last thing here I want you to note. Let me show you what it is by plotting the
components:

```
fig_a2 = model_a.plot_components(forecast_a)
plt.show()
```

This plots the components for our `model_a` with additive seasonality:

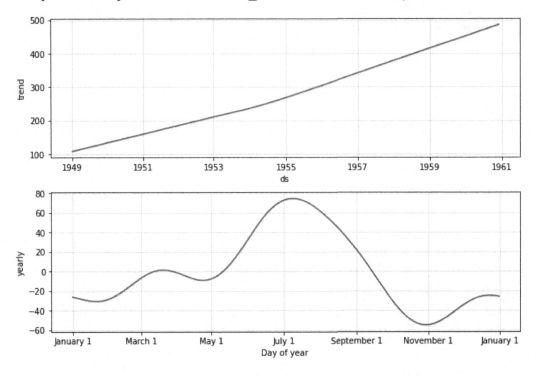

Figure 4.4 – Components plot with additive seasonality

And now, let's plot the components for `model_m`:

```
fig_m2 = model_m.plot_components(forecast_m)
plt.show()
```

Compare this next plot with the previous plot in *Figure 4.4*:

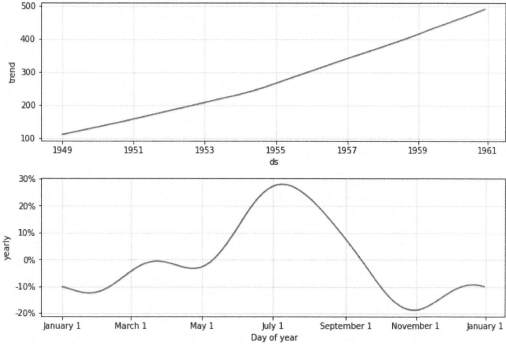

Figure 4.5 – Components plot with multiplicative seasonality

They look almost identical. The trend is the same, starting in **1949** just above **100** and rising to just below **500** by **1961**, with a slight kink in **1954** where the trend accelerates. The yearly seasonality behaves as we might expect, with the peak number of air passengers occurring in the summer and smaller local peaks over the Christmas holidays and Spring Break. The difference between the two charts is the *y*-axis of the seasonality curve.

In the additive model, the *y*-axis values are absolute numbers. In the multiplicative model, they are a percentage. This is because with an additive seasonality mode, the seasonality is modeled as an additional factor to the trend, simply adding or subtracting values from it. But in the multiplicative seasonality mode, the seasonality represents a relative deviation from the trend, so the magnitude of the seasonality effect will depend on what value the trend is predicting at that point; the seasonality effect is a percentage of the trend.

> **Tip**
>
> When your data represents a count of something over time, such as the count of airline passengers each month, you will very often model it with multiplicative seasonality. Using additive seasonality can cause negative values to be predicted (negative 100 passengers per month, for example, is not possible), whereas multiplicative seasonality will merely shrink values closer to zero.

Choosing additive versus multiplicative seasonality can be a bit tricky at first, but if you just remember the insight that the seasonality may be an absolute factor or a relative factor and observe whether the *spread* of the data is constant or not, you should have no trouble with your models.

Now that you understand the difference between these two seasonality modes, let's apply it to a new dataset, Divvy bike share, and continue learning about seasonality in Prophet.

In many examples throughout this book, we will be creating examples using data from the Divvy bike share program in Chicago. In the previous chapter, we used hourly Divvy data, but in this section, we will use daily data.

> **Tip**
>
> We used the hourly Divvy data in *Chapter 3, Non-Daily Data*, to demonstrate both the *daily* component plot and how to work with regular gaps in the data, and we will use the hourly data again in this chapter when we look at conditional seasonalities. But otherwise, throughout this book, we will be using the daily Divvy data, which is presented here. In these cases, we don't need the extra granularity of the hourly data and changing to daily data reduces processing time from minutes down to seconds. Furthermore, the daily dataset has associated weather and temperature columns, which are lacking in the hourly dataset, which we will use in *Chapter 8, Additional Regressors*.

Here is what the daily Divvy data looks like:

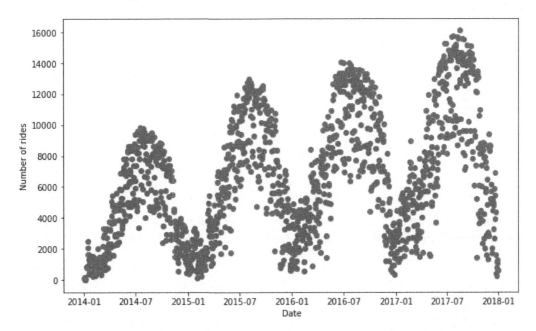

Figure 4.6 – Number of rides per day on Divvy

This is count data, because it represents the number of rides each day, and you can also see that the magnitude of the seasonality is growing with the trend (if we plotted those dotted lines from *Figure 4.1*, tracing the upper and lower bounds of the data, the lines would be diverging). As we just learned, these are an indication of multiplicative seasonality, so let's be sure to set that when instantiating our model. We imported the necessary Python libraries in the previous example, so we can begin this example by loading the data.

This dataset contains some additional columns for weather and temperature conditions, which we will be using to enrich our forecast in *Chapter 8, Additional Regressors*. Once we load the data, you can see these additional columns:

```
df = pd.read_csv('divvy_daily.csv')
df.head()
```

Running that command in a Jupyter Notebook or IPython instance reveals the following
DataFrame:

	date	rides	temperature	weather
0	1/1/2014	95	19.483158	rain or snow
1	1/2/2014	111	16.833333	rain or snow
2	1/3/2014	6	-5.633333	clear
3	1/4/2014	181	30.007735	rain or snow
4	1/5/2014	32	16.756250	rain or snow

Figure 4.7 – The Divvy DataFrame

For now, though, we only need the date and rides columns. Let's load those into our
Prophet DataFrame with the appropriate column names. We will work with weather
and temperature in *Chapter 8, Additional Regressors*:

```
df = df[['date', 'rides']]
df['date'] = pd.to_datetime(df['date'])
df.columns = ['ds', 'y']
```

As before, we need to create an instance of the Prophet class before calling the fit
method. Note that we are setting seasonality_mode to 'multiplicative'
because we noticed when plotting the raw data that the seasonality fluctuations were
growing with the increasing trend. After fitting the model, we will again create a future
DataFrame, with a one-year forecast, and then call predict to create the forecast
DataFrame and send it to the plot method:

```
model = Prophet(seasonality_mode='multiplicative')
model.fit(df)
future = model.make_future_dataframe(periods=365)
forecast = model.predict(future)
fig = model.plot(forecast)
plt.show()
```

After running that code, you should find that Prophet has created the following plot:

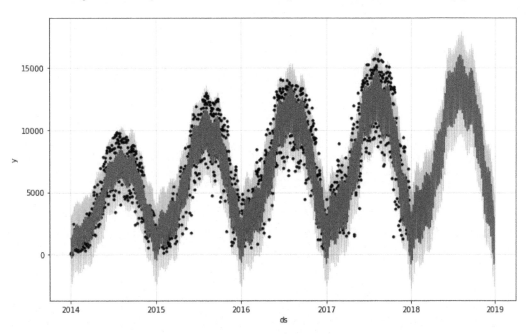

Figure 4.8 – Divvy forecast

We can see that the predicted trend is indeed increasing along with the actual data and that the yearly seasonality also matches. Let's now plot our components and see what they reveal:

```
fig2 = model.plot_components(forecast)
plt.show()
```

As you can see in the output plot, Prophet has isolated three components in this dataset: the **trend**, a **weekly** seasonality, and a **yearly** seasonality:

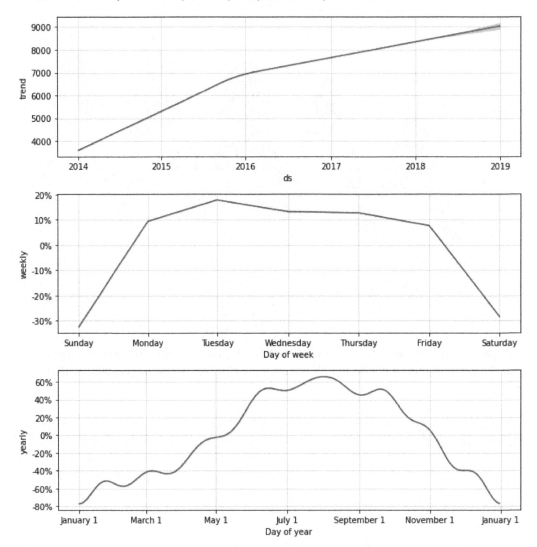

Figure 4.9 – Divvy components plot

By default, Prophet will identify a **yearly** seasonality whenever the `'ds'` column contains at least two full years of data. **Weekly** seasonality will be included when there are at least two weeks of data and the spacing between dates is less than seven days. There is also a default daily seasonality, which we saw in the previous chapter, which would be included if the dataset both contained at least two days of data (which of course in this case it does) and the spacing between rows in the `'ds'` column is less than one day (which fails in this case).

The trend linearly increases relatively rapidly for the first two years but then bends and slows slightly for the remaining two years, and the forecasted year continues to follow this slope. We can see that the Divvy network has grown in average usage over this time period from about 3500 rides per day in 2014 to about 8500 per day by the end of 2018.

The weekly seasonality shows that there are about 30% fewer rides per day on the weekends—maybe all these riders are work commuters—with rides on the weekdays being 10–20% higher than the trend would indicate. This fits our intuition that weekdays and weekends could reasonably show a different pattern.

Now, looking at the yearly seasonality reveals that rides in the summer are about 60% higher than the trend, while rides in the winter are 80% lower. Again, this also intuitively makes sense. Those work commuters are going to drive or take public transport when the weather gets cold and rainy.

You'll notice that this yearly seasonality curve is quite *wavy*, just as we noticed in the previous chapter with the hourly Divvy data. You may have expected a much smoother curve, not one with so many inflection points. This is a result of our yearly seasonality being too flexible, it has too many **degrees of freedom**, or too many mathematical parameters controlling the curve. In Prophet, the number of parameters controlling the seasonality curve is called the **Fourier order**.

Controlling seasonality with Fourier order

Seasonality is at the heart of how Prophet works, and Fourier series are how seasonality is modeled. To understand what a Fourier series is, and how the Fourier order relates to it, I'll use an analogy from linear regression.

You may know that increasing the order of a polynomial equation in linear regression will always improve your goodness-of-fit. For example, the simple linear regression equation is $y = \beta_1 x + \beta_0$, with $\beta 1$ being the slope of the line and $\beta 0$ the y-intercept. Increasing the order of your equation to, say, $y = \beta_2 x^2 + \beta_1 x + \beta_0$ will always improve your fit, at the risk of overfitting and capturing noise. You can always achieve an $R2$ value of 1 (perfect fit) by arbitrarily increasing the order of your polynomial equation higher and higher. The following figure illustrates how higher-order fits start to become quite unrealistic and overfit, though:

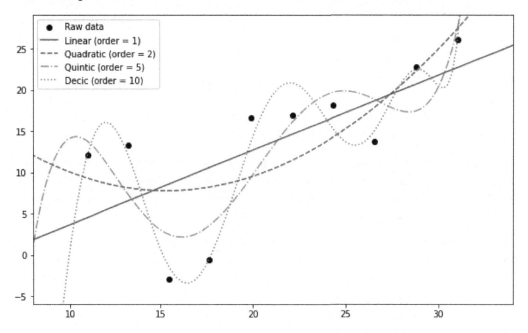

Figure 4.10 – Linear regression with higher-order polynomials

The linear solid line does get the upward trend of the data correct, but it seems to be missing some subtle detail. The **Quadratic** dashed line is a better fit (indeed, this data was simulated from a quadratic equation with random noise). But the **Quintic** and **Decic** curves are clearly overfitting to the random noise. If we sample some more data points from this distribution, they will most likely cause the **Quintic** and **Decic** curves to radically change to fit the new data, whereas the **Linear** and **Quadratic** curves will only shift slightly. We may say that the order of a polynomial is proportional to the number of bends the curve can take in order to fit the data.

A Fourier series is simply a sum of sine waves. By changing the shape of these individual sine waves—the amplitude, or height of the wave; the period, or distance from peak-to-peak; and the phase, or where along the length of the wave the cycle begins—we can create a new and very complex wave shape.

In the linear domain, we changed the order of the polynomial to control the amount of flexibility the curve has, and we changed the β coefficients to control the actual shape of the curve. Similarly, in the periodic domain, we change the number of sine waves in our Fourier series—this is the Fourier order—to control the flexibility of the final curve and we (or, more accurately, Prophet's fitting equations) change the amplitude, period, and phase of the individual waves to control the actual shape of our final curve. You can see how this summation works in the following figure:

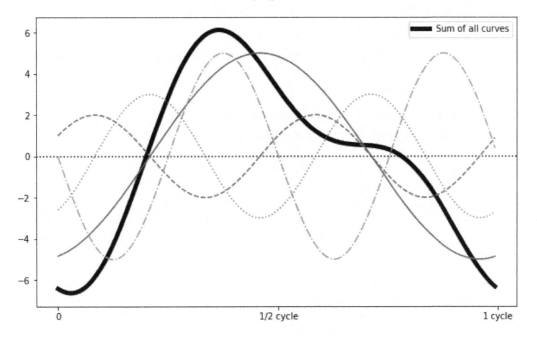

Figure 4.11 – Fourier series of order 4

The solid line is simply the sum of each of the four sine waves. By arbitrarily increasing the Fourier order in our model, we can always achieve a perfect fit for any set of data. But just as in the linear domain, this approach will inevitably lead to overfitting.

Remember in *Figure 4.9* when we plotted the components of the Divvy forecast and the yearly seasonality was too wavy? This is the result of a Fourier order being too high. By default, Prophet fits yearly seasonality with an order of 10, weekly seasonality with an order of 3, and daily seasonality (if sub-daily data is provided, of course) of 4. Usually, these defaults work very well and no tuning is needed. However, in Divvy's case, we do need to reduce the Fourier order of the yearly seasonality in order to achieve a better fit with the data. Let's see how to do that.

We already have our necessary libraries imported and the data loaded into our df DataFrame from the previous example, so to continue, we need to instantiate a new Prophet object with a modified yearly seasonality. As before, we will set the seasonality mode to multiplicative, but this time we will include the yearly_seasonality argument and set it to 4. This is where we set the Fourier order.

You may experiment with different values on your own; I have found 4 to provide a clean curve without much flexibility in most cases, which is what I want here. Similarly, if we wanted to change the Fourier order of weekly_seasonality or daily_ seasonality, we would do so here.

After instantiating our model, we merely need to fit it on the data in order to plot the seasonality. There is no need to predict in this case:

```
model = Prophet(seasonality_mode='multiplicative',
                yearly_seasonality=4)
model.fit(df)
```

We will use a new function here to plot just the yearly component, the plot_yearly function from Prophet's plot package. We need to import it first:

```
from fbprophet.plot import plot_yearly
```

Note that there is also a plot_weekly function, which operates much the same way. Both functions require the first argument to be the model; here, we will also include the optional figure size argument so as to match the scale of our previous plot contained in *Figure 4.9*:

```
fig3 = plot_yearly(model, figsize=(10.5, 3.25))
plt.show()
```

Compare this output with the yearly seasonality curve in *Figure 4.9*:

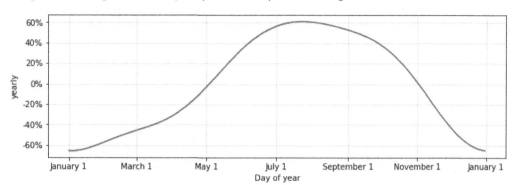

Figure 4.12 – Divvy yearly seasonality with a Fourier order of 4

We have successfully eliminated the waviness of our previous attempt, while still maintaining the clear shape of the seasonality. This seems much more reasonable!

So far, we have only been working with Prophet's default seasonalities. Obviously, though, there are many cyclic datasets out there with periods that don't fall neatly into the yearly, weekly, or daily seasonality bins. Prophet supports custom seasonalities precisely for this purpose. Let's check them out in the next section.

Adding custom seasonalities

So far, the only seasonalities we have worked with are the defaults in Prophet: yearly, weekly, and daily. But there is no reason to limit ourselves to these seasonalities. If your data contains a cycle that is either longer or shorter than the 365.25-day yearly cycle, the 7-day weekly cycle, or the 1-day daily cycle, Prophet makes it easy to model this seasonality yourself.

A great example of a non-standard seasonality is the 11-year cycle of sunspots. Sunspots are regions on the Sun's surface that temporarily exhibit a much-reduced temperature, and hence appear much darker, than surrounding areas.

Beginning in approximately 1609, Galileo Galilei began systematic observation of sunspots and over the last 400+ years, this phenomenon has been constantly recorded. In fact, sunspots represent the longest continuously recorded time series of any natural phenomenon. Through these observations, scientists have identified a quasi-periodic cycle of 11 years during which the frequency of sunspot occurrences varies. They say *quasi*-periodic because the cycle length seems to vary from cycle to cycle—it isn't perfectly 11 years each time. The average cycle length is 11 years though, so that is what we will use to model it.

The **Solar Influences Data analysis Center** (**SIDC**), a department of the Royal Observatory of Belgium in Brussels, makes available a dataset of sunspot activity from 1750 to the present day in their **World Data Center – Sunspot Index and Long-term Solar Observations** (**WDC-SILSO**) project. This dataset will be a good demonstration of how to add a new seasonality to Prophet. We begin by loading our data:

```
df = pd.read_csv('sunspots.csv',\
                 usecols=['Date', 'Monthly Mean Total\
                 Sunspot Number'])
df['Date'] = pd.to_datetime(df['Date'])
df.columns = ['ds', 'y']
```

Let's visualize this data to see how it looks:

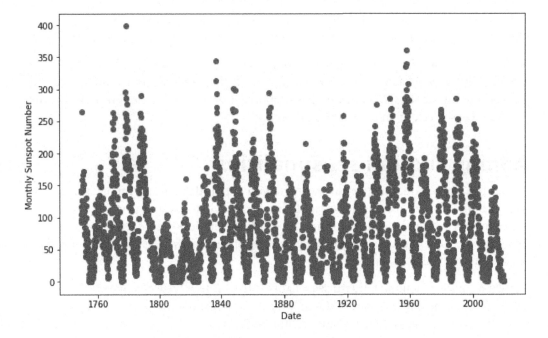

Figure 4.13 – Number of sunspots per month

The data appears rather noisy; there appear to be a number of outliers and the cycle is not perfectly clean. There is quite a lot of variation in the peak of each cycle. To see how Prophet will handle this data, we first need to instantiate our model. This is count data, so we will choose multiplicative seasonality.

Another consideration we will take is that the Sun is so large that it hardly feels the minuscule tug of Earth's gravity as we orbit around our star; therefore, the Sun does not experience what we would call a yearly seasonality at all. We will instruct Prophet not to attempt to fit a yearly seasonality. Prophet won't attempt a weekly or daily seasonality because we are providing monthly data.

We learned how to adjust the Fourier order of the yearly seasonality earlier in this chapter by passing an integer to the `yearly_seasonality` argument. This is the same argument we use to turn off a default seasonality; simply pass a Boolean instead. We pass `yearly_seasonality=False` to instruct Prophet not to fit yearly seasonality:

```
model = Prophet(seasonality_mode='multiplicative',
                yearly_seasonality=False)
```

Once our model is instantiated, we can add seasonalities. We do this with the `add_seasonality` method. The method requires that we pass arguments for the name of the seasonality (we'll call this one `'11-year cycle'`), the period (11 years times 365.25 days, as `period` is stated in days), and Fourier order (we'll use 5 in this case, but feel free to experiment). This is how it all looks together:

```
model.add_seasonality(name='11-year cycle',
                      period=11 * 365.25,
                      fourier_order=5)
```

Stating the period can be tricky; just remember that it is always counted in days. So, a seasonality longer than a day will have a number greater than 1 and a seasonality shorter than a day will have a period less than 1.

The rest of this example is exactly as in previous ones; we fit on the training DataFrame, create a future DataFrame, and then predict on it:

```
model.fit(df)
future = model.make_future_dataframe(periods=240, freq='M')
forecast = model.predict(future)
fig2 = model.plot_components(forecast)
plt.show()
```

Let's inspect the components plot to see what we created:

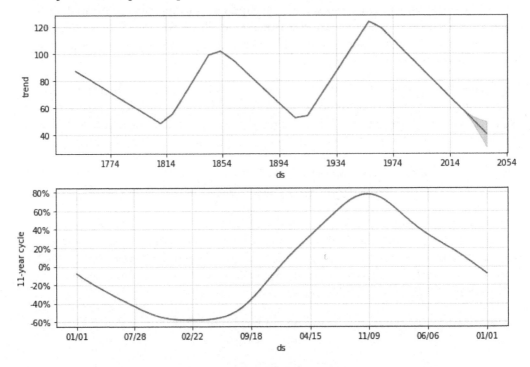

Figure 4.14 – Sunspots components plot

The plot shows just the trend and the 11-year cycle, exactly what we expected. The trend has a sawtooth shape; in fact, scientists have named that trough around 1814 the *Dalton Minimum*, named after the English meteorologist John Dalton. The peak during the 1950s is called the *Modern Maximum*. But it's the 11-year cycle that we're interested in here.

The x-axis can be a bit confusing because it only contains the month and year, but each tick is about 1.5 years later than the previous tick. The whole cycle is indeed 11 years. We can see that the low point is a bit *flatter* than the high point and has about 60% fewer sunspots than the average. The high point sees about 80% more sunspots than average.

To see all of the seasonalities that your model currently has, as well as the parameters controlling that seasonality, simply call the `seasonalities` attribute of the model:

```
model.seasonalities
```

This outputs a dictionary where the keys are the names of the seasonalities and the values are the parameters. In this example, where we only have one seasonality, this is the output dictionary:

```
OrderedDict([('11-year cycle',
            {'period': 4017.75,
             'fourier_order': 5,
             'prior_scale': 10.0,
             'mode': 'multiplicative',
             'condition_name': None})])
```

> **Important note**
>
> When specifying a period for your seasonality, it is always specified in days. So, a 10-year seasonality will have a period of 10 (years) x 365.25 (days per year) = 3652.5 days. An hourly seasonality would be 1 (day) / 24 (hours per day) = 0.04167 days.
>
> Be careful not to confuse the period of seasonality with the period used in `make_future_dataframe`. The period in seasonality is always specified in days, while the period in `make_future_dataframe` is specified by the `freq` argument.

Adding a seasonality to Prophet that doesn't actually exist in the data can cause Prophet to be very slow to fit, as it struggles to find a pattern where none exists and can actually harm your forecast as Prophet will eventually fit the non-existent seasonality to noise. However, other seasonalities you may find yourself frequently adding may be an hourly seasonality, if your data is measured per minute, as follows:

```
model.add_seasonality(name='hourly',
                      # an hour is 0.04167 days
                      period=1 / 24,
                      # experiment with this value
                      fourier_order=5)
```

A seasonality for the quarterly business cycle would be created in the following manner:

```
model.add_seasonality(name='quarterly',
                      # a quarter is 91.3125 days
                      period=365.25 / 4
                      # experiment with this value
                      fourier_order=5)
```

That's how you add custom seasonalities! We'll be using this `add_seasonality` method a bit more in this chapter, starting with this next section about seasonalities that depend on other factors.

Adding conditional seasonalities

Suppose you work for a utility company in a college town and are tasked with forecasting the electricity usage for the coming year. The electricity usage is going to depend upon the population of the town to some extent, and as a college town, there are thousands of students who are only temporary residents! How do you set up Prophet to handle this scenario? Conditional seasonalities exist for this purpose.

Conditional seasonalities are those that are in effect for only a portion of the dates in the training and future DataFrames. A conditional seasonality must have a cycle that is shorter than the period in which it is active. So, for example, it wouldn't make sense to have a yearly seasonality that is active for just a few months.

Forecasting electricity usage in the college town would require you to set up either daily or weekly seasonalities—and possibly even both, depending upon the usage patterns, one daily/weekly seasonality for the summer months when students have returned to their hometowns, and another daily/weekly seasonality for the rest of the year. Ideally, the conditional seasonality would have at least two full cycles each time it is active.

To learn how to build a conditional seasonality, we will go back to the hourly Divvy data that we explored in the previous chapter. Based on the weekly seasonality we observed in that example, we know ridership is significantly lower on weekends than weekdays, suggesting most riders are commuting to work.

We saw in the daily seasonality plot that ridership has usage peaks around 8 a.m. and 6 p.m., during the morning and evening rush hours. This may lead you to suspect that the usage throughout the day will follow different patterns on a weekday versus the weekend. That is, maybe those peaks we see at 8 a.m. and 6 p.m. and the midday trough will all disappear on weekends, with activity levels more even throughout the day. To test this hypothesis, let's build a forecast model using different daily seasonalities for weekends than for weekdays.

The basic procedure for adding this conditional seasonality is to add new Boolean columns to your training DataFrame (and later, matching columns in the future DataFrame) indicating whether that row is a weekend or weekday. Then, disable the default weekly seasonality and add two new weekly seasonalities that specify those new Boolean columns as conditions. Let's see how to do this.

We have the necessary libraries already loaded, so to begin, we need to create our Prophet DataFrame using the Divvy hourly data:

```
df = pd.read_csv('divvy_hourly.csv')
df['date'] = pd.to_datetime(df['date'])
df.columns = ['ds', 'y']
```

Now, this is where we identify the condition for our seasonality. Let's create a function that outputs `True` if the given date is on a weekend and `False` otherwise. Then, we'll use `pandas'` `apply` method to create a new column for weekends and use the tilde (~) operator to take the inverse results for another new column for weekdays. Finally, let's output the first few rows of our DataFrame at this point just so that we can see what we've got:

```
def is_weekend(ds):
    date = pd.to_datetime(ds)
    return (date.dayofweek == 5 or date.dayofweek == 6)


df['weekend'] = df['ds'].apply(is_weekend)
df['weekday'] = ~df['ds'].apply(is_weekend)


df.head()
```

If your functions correctly identified the days, you should see this output:

	ds	y	weekend	weekday
0	2014-01-01 01:00:00	1	False	True
1	2014-01-01 02:00:00	9	False	True
2	2014-01-01 03:00:00	4	False	True
3	2014-01-01 04:00:00	1	False	True
4	2014-01-01 07:00:00	2	False	True

Figure 4.15 – The Divvy conditional seasonality DataFrame

January 1, 2014 was a Wednesday, so that output matches what we would expect. Next, we need to instantiate our model. Using what we learned earlier in this chapter, we set the seasonality mode to `multiplicative`, as this Divvy data represents count values. We will also set the Fourier order of both yearly and weekly seasonalities to 6; my testing showed that to be a good value on this dataset. Finally, because we are adding conditional daily seasonalities, we will disable the default daily seasonality:

```
model = Prophet(seasonality_mode='multiplicative',
                yearly_seasonality=6,
                weekly_seasonality=6,
                daily_seasonality=False)
```

To create conditional seasonalities, we use the same `add_seasonality` method that we learned about while modeling the sunspot cycle, but in this case, we will use the optional `condition_name` argument to specify that the new seasonality is conditional.

The `condition_name` argument must be passed the name of a column in the training DataFrame consisting of Boolean values identifying which rows to apply the seasonality to—our weekend and weekday columns. Just as we did in the sunspots example, we also need to name the seasonality and identify both the period and Fourier order:

```
model.add_seasonality(name='daily_weekend',
                      period=1,
                      fourier_order=3,
                      condition_name='weekend')
model.add_seasonality(name='daily_weekday',
                      period=1,
                      fourier_order=3,
                      condition_name='weekday')
```

That's it for setting up the model! We will next fit the model on our training data and create the `future` DataFrame just as before, being careful to set the frequency to *hourly* now that we are using hourly data. The last step in setting up conditional seasonalities is to identify where in the future DataFrame the condition will apply.

We already created the `is_weekend` function and applied it to our training DataFrame, `df`. We simply need to repeat that procedure on the `future` DataFrame before calling `predict` to create our forecast:

```
model.fit(df)
future = model.make_future_dataframe(periods=365 * 24,
                                      freq='h')
future['weekend'] = future['ds'].apply(is_weekend)
future['weekday'] = ~future['ds'].apply(is_weekend)
forecast = model.predict(future)
```

We named our two conditional seasonalities `'daily_weekend'` and `'daily_weekday'`, so let's import the `plot_seasonality` function, which we discovered in the previous chapter, and plot these two seasonalities:

```
from fbprophet.plot import plot_seasonality

fig3 = plot_seasonality(model, 'daily_weekday',
                        figsize=(10, 3))
plt.show()
fig4 = plot_seasonality(model, 'daily_weekend',
                        figsize=(10, 3))
plt.show()
```

If everything ran correctly, you should have two new plots:

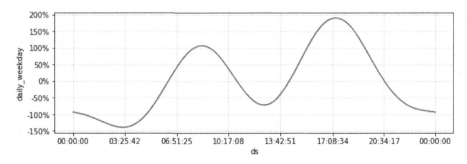

Figure 4.16 – Daily weekday component plot

On weekdays, the trend appears much the same as we saw when we used the default daily seasonality—a peak around 8 a.m., another peak around 6 p.m., and a small hump just after midnight. Our hypothesis was that weekends would see a much different pattern though. Let's look at the plot to see:

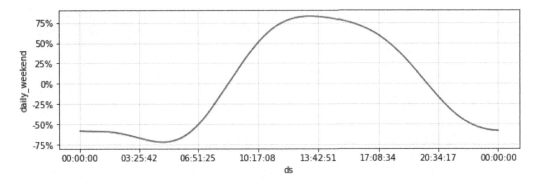

Figure 4.17 – Daily weekend component plot

And indeed, we do see a difference! As your intuition might have suggested, on the weekends Divvy riders tend to get a later start than on weekdays, with a gradual increase in ridership up until noon and then a gradual decrease all the way to midnight. There is no midday slump as we saw on working days.

So far in this chapter, you used the Air Passengers data to learn the difference between additive and multiplicative seasonality. Later, you used the Divvy data to learn how to add custom seasonalities and conditional seasonalities. You also used Divvy data to discover the Fourier order and learned how to control the flexibility of the seasonality curve. There is another lever Prophet makes available to you to control seasonality: regularization.

Regularizing seasonality

Often, when solving a problem with machine learning, the data involved is so complex that a simple model just isn't powerful enough to capture the full subtlety of the patterns to be found. The simple model tends to **underfit** the data. In contrast, a more complicated model with many parameters and great flexibility can tend to **overfit** the data. It is not always easy, or possible, to use a simpler model. In these cases, **regularization** is a good technique to use in order to control overfitting.

Prophet is such a powerful forecasting tool that without care, it can sometimes be very easy to overfit the data. That's why understanding Prophet's regularization parameters can be quite useful.

> **Tip**
>
> A model is said to be *underfit* if it does not fully capture the true relationship between the input features and the output features. Performance is low on both the training data and any unseen testing data.
>
> A model is said to be *overfit* if it goes beyond capturing the true relationship and begins to capture random trends in the noise of the data. Performance can be very high on the training data but low on the unseen testing data.
>
> A model with a good fit will perform equally well on both training and testing data.

Regularization is a technique for controlling overfitting by forcing a model to be less flexible. For example, in *Figure 3.7*, I simulated a set of points with random noise (the true relationship I used is $y = (x - 20)^2 + 50$) and fit two lines using 8th-degree polynomial regression (in reality, you would rarely choose such a high order for a regression model; I am using it here merely to exaggerate the point). One line is not regularized at all, and the other is:

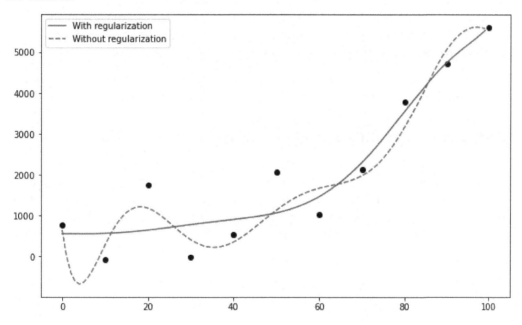

Figure 4.18 – Regularization effects

As you can see in the plot, the unregularized line is overfit and wiggles around the true relationship while attempting to fit to the noise. By regularizing, in contrast, the flexibility of the line is constrained and it is forced to trace out a much smoother curve. With the true curve essentially being $y = x^2$, it is clear that the regularized line, while still not perfect, does a better job of approximating the relationship and will perform better on new data.

The full Prophet package has several adjustable parameters for regularization. For seasonality, that parameter is called the prior scale.

In statistics, you may have an uncertain quantity that you intend to find the value of. The **prior probability distribution**, often just called a prior, of that quantity is the probability distribution of values you would expect *prior to* learning some bit of additional information.

For example, let's say I ask you to guess the height of a specific human male. In your mind, you imagine all the likely heights of males. That range of heights is the prior probability distribution. Next, I tell you that the male is an NBA basketball player. You know basketball players are typically much taller than the average male, so you update that distribution to skew more toward tall heights because the additional information I provided you with better informs your guess.

The prior is your starting point, what you believe to be true before receiving additional information. Let's see how to apply this idea to seasonality in Prophet.

Global seasonality regularization

The first way to apply seasonality regularization is globally, affecting all seasonalities in your model equally. `seasonality_prior_scale` is an attribute of your Prophet model instance and is set when you instantiate your model. If you do not set it, the default will be `10`. Reducing this number will apply more regularization, which will rein in your model's seasonalities. Let's see this in action.

We'll use the Divvy daily data in this example, so we need to begin by loading it into our Prophet DataFrame, as the necessary libraries should already be loaded from previous examples:

```
df = pd.read_csv('divvy_daily.csv')
df = df[['date', 'rides']]
df['date'] = pd.to_datetime(df['date'])
df.columns = ['ds', 'y']
```

Now, we need to instantiate our model, setting the seasonality mode to multiplicative. While learning about Fourier order, you went through a forecast with this dataset using the default `seasonality_prior_scale` value of 10. So, let's use a prior scale this time around of 0.01. We also found the yearly seasonality to be better modeled with a Fourier order of 4, so we'll set that as well. You can refer back to *Figure 4.8* and *Figure 4.9* to see the unregularized model for comparison:

```
model = Prophet(seasonality_mode='multiplicative',
                yearly_seasonality=4,
                seasonality_prior_scale=.01)
```

With the regularization set, all that is left to do is complete the model as we did earlier:

```
model.fit(df)
future = model.make_future_dataframe(periods=365)
forecast = model.predict(future)
fig = model.plot(forecast)
plt.show()
fig2 = model.plot_components(forecast)
plt.show()
```

First, we will look at the forecast, and then the components:

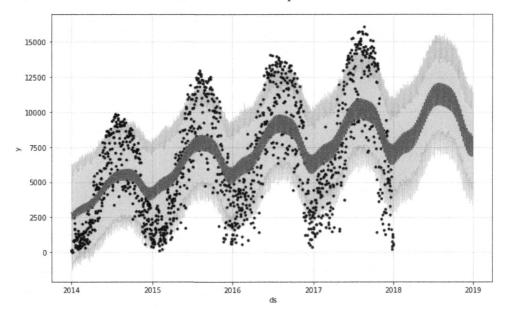

Figure 4.19 – Regularized forecast

Comparing *Figure 4.19* with *Figure 4.8* shows that the seasonal swings in our forecast have indeed been dampened. Both the annual seasonality and the weekly seasonality show less variation. The uncertainty intervals between the two models are roughly the same though, because the variance in the data is now handled in the Prophet model's noise term instead of the seasonality term.

Now, let's look at the components plot:

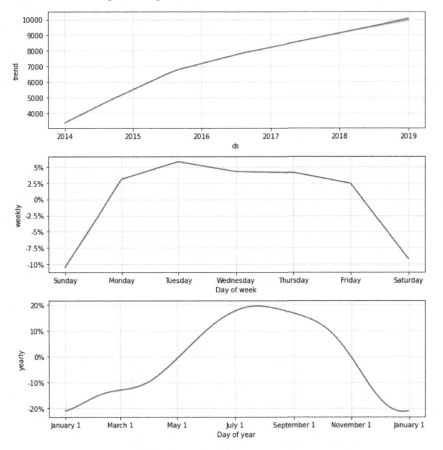

Figure 4.20 – Regularized components plot

Comparing this figure with *Figure 4.9*, we see that the trend is very similar. We only constrained the seasonality, not the trend at all. The trend did change a bit (the peak value is a bit higher) because Prophet is attempting to capture some of the seasonal variations with the trend, but the shape is nearly identical. The weekly and yearly seasonalities appear the same, but their y-axes show the magnitudes have been reduced in the range of one third to one quarter of their regularized levels. This is the effect of seasonality regularization: it reduces the magnitude of the curve's values.

To illustrate the effect of different seasonality prior scales, let's compare the yearly and weekly seasonality curves of this dataset when modeled with different prior scales. First, here is the yearly seasonality plot:

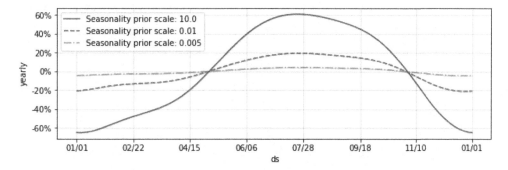

Figure 4.21 – Yearly seasonality with different prior scales

And here is the weekly seasonality plot:

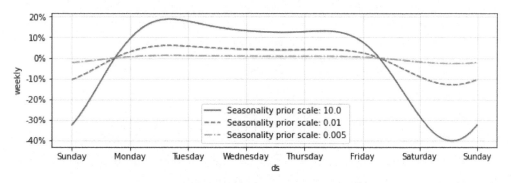

Figure 4.22 – Weekly seasonality with different prior scales

The solid line in both plots is the default scale of 10; the dashed line and dashed-dotted line show increasing regularization amounts. Whereas modifying the Fourier order helped control the seasonality curve by reducing the number of bends it was allowed to take, modifying the seasonality prior scale helps control seasonality by reducing the amount of variation it is able to achieve.

In this section, you have learned how to regularize all seasonalities at the same time. Next, let's see how to regularize the seasonalities individually.

Local seasonality regularization

Let's say that you are happy with the yearly seasonality curve with the default regularization setting, but your weekly curve is too extreme and overfitting. In that case, you can use the add_seasonality method to create a new weekly seasonality with a custom prior scale.

Let's continue on and instantiate a new model, again with multiplicative seasonality and a Fourier order of 4 applied to the yearly seasonality. This time though, we will be adding a new weekly seasonality, so let's remove the default by setting it to False while instantiating:

```
model = Prophet(seasonality_mode='multiplicative',
                yearly_seasonality=4,
                weekly_seasonality=False)
```

As you learned in the section on custom seasonalities, we will now add a seasonality with a period of 7 days and name it 'weekly'. We are happy with the default weekly Fourier order of 4, so we'll use that again here, but we want more regularization than is the default, so we use the prior_scale argument to set it to 0.01:

```
model.add_seasonality(name='weekly',
                      period=7,
                      fourier_order=4,
                      prior_scale=0.01)
```

Now, as I hope is becoming second nature to you, we will fit the model and predict on the future DataFrame. Let's just plot the components this time:

```
model.fit(df)
future = model.make_future_dataframe(periods=365)
forecast = model.predict(future)
fig2 = model.plot_components(forecast)
plt.show()
```

You should see this plot, which looks nearly identical to *Figure 4.20*:

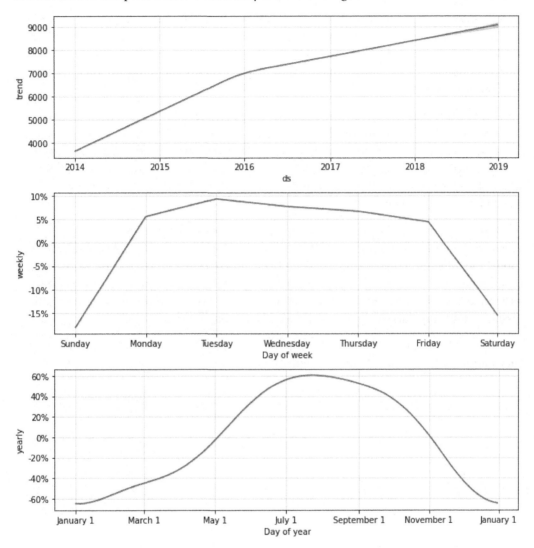

Figure 4.23 – Weekly regularized components plot

You'll now see that the magnitude of the unregularized yearly seasonality matches that of *Figure 4.9*, but the regularized weekly seasonality is reduced by about half, as expected. All of your seasonalities can have different regularization strengths applied, simply with repeated `add_seasonality` calls. Reasonable values for these prior scales range from about 10 down to around 0.01.

Summary

Seasonality truly is the heart of Facebook Prophet. This chapter covered a lot of ground; the foundations you learned here will be used throughout the remaining chapters of this book. Indeed, almost any model you build in Prophet will have seasonality considerations, whereas many of the upcoming chapters cover special cases that may or may not apply to your specific problem.

You started this chapter by learning the difference between additive and multiplicative seasonality, and how to identify whether your dataset features one or the other. We then briefly discussed Fourier series and demonstrated how a partial Fourier sum can build a very complex periodic curve. Using these ideas, you learned how setting the Fourier order of a seasonality can be used to control its shape by allowing either more or less freedom to bend along its path.

Next, you modeled the 11-year cycle of sunspots and learned how to add custom seasonalities. These custom seasonalities came into use again when you learned how to model the different weekday and weekend behaviors of riders on Divvy's network using conditional seasonalities. Finally, we looked at regularization techniques, both globally as applied to all seasonalities together and locally, using yet again the custom seasonalities lesson to apply regularization to just the weekly seasonality alone.

In the next chapter, you will learn all about holidays in the Prophet package, which among many topics will also include more detail about regularization as it applies to Prophet.

5
Holidays

Because Prophet was designed to handle business forecasting cases, it is important to include the effects of holidays, which naturally play a large role in business activities. Just as bike-share commuters will ride more frequently in the summer than the winter, or on Tuesdays than on Sundays, it is reasonable to hypothesize that they would ride less than otherwise expected on Thanksgiving, for example.

Fortunately, Prophet includes robust support for including the effects of holidays in your forecasts. Furthermore, the techniques Prophet has for including the effects of holidays can be used to add any holiday-like event, such as the food festival that we will model in this chapter.

Similar to the seasonality effects you learned about in the previous chapter, Prophet contains default holidays that you can apply to your models, as well as custom holidays that you can create yourself. This chapter will cover both situations. Additionally, you will learn how to control the strength of holiday effects using the technique that you learned with seasonality: regularization.

In this chapter, you will learn how to go about doing the following:

- Adding default country holidays
- Adding default state or province holidays
- Creating custom holidays

- Creating multi-day holidays
- Regularizing holidays

Technical requirements

The data files and code for the examples in this chapter can be found at `https://github.com/PacktPublishing/Forecasting-Time-Series-Data-with-Facebook-Prophet`.

Adding default country holidays

Prophet uses the Python `holidays` package to populate a default list of holidays by country and, optionally, by state or province. To specify which region to build a holiday list for, Prophet requires the name or ISO code of that country. A complete list of all countries available, with their ISO codes, and also any states or provinces that can be included, can be viewed in the package's README file here: `https://github.com/dr-prodigy/python-holidays#available-countries`.

To add the default holidays, Prophet includes an `add_country_holidays` method, which simply takes the ISO code for that country. Let's walk through an example using the Divvy dataset again, first adding holidays for the United States, and then including a few additional holidays specific to Illinois, as Divvy is located in Chicago.

We begin just as we have learned to do with our other models in this book, by importing the necessary libraries, loading our data, and instantiating our model. As you learned how to do in *Chapter 4, Seasonality*, we will set the seasonality mode to multiplicative and the yearly seasonality to a Fourier order of 4:

```
import pandas as pd
import matplotlib.pyplot as plt
from fbprophet import Prophet

df = pd.read_csv('divvy_daily.csv')
df = df[['date', 'rides']]
df['date'] = pd.to_datetime(df['date'])
df.columns = ['ds', 'y']

model = Prophet(seasonality_mode='multiplicative',
                yearly_seasonality=4)
```

This next line is all that is required to populate the model with a list of holidays for the United States:

```
model.add_country_holidays(country_name='US')
```

Now, to complete the model, all we need to do is call `fit` as usual on the training DataFrame, make our future DataFrame, and call `predict` on it. We will plot the forecast and components to view our results:

```
model.fit(df)
future = model.make_future_dataframe(periods=365)
forecast = model.predict(future)
fig = model.plot(forecast)
plt.show()
```

The output forecast plot looks very similar to the *Figure 4.7* plot from *Chapter 4, Seasonality*:

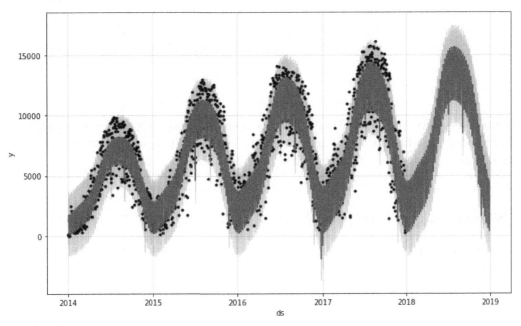

Figure 5.1 – Divvy forecast including US holidays

However, the eagle-eyed may notice some downward spikes around the middle of the year and the end of the year. To discern what those are, we look at the components plot as follows:

```
fig2 = model.plot_components(forecast)
plt.show()
```

In the output of those commands, the trend and both weekly and yearly seasonalities are again included and look much the same. However, there is a new plot shown: holidays, as seen here (note that the preceding code produces a full components plot; the following figure is a crop of that image):

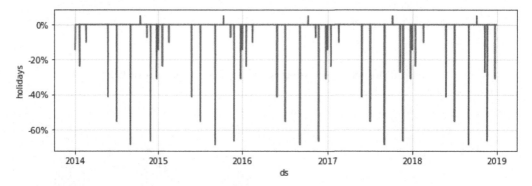

Figure 5.2 – Divvy US holidays component

This shows spikes where Divvy usage deviates from the trend, each spike corresponding to a holiday. Each holiday shows decreased usage except for one, which occurs in the final quarter of each year. Let's investigate this.

We can view the holidays included in our model with this command:

```
model.train_holiday_names
```

This outputs a Python object containing an index and the holiday names included in the model:

```
0                        New Year's Day
1           Martin Luther King Jr. Day
2               Washington's Birthday
3                        Memorial Day
4                    Independence Day
5                          Labor Day
6                       Columbus Day
7                       Veterans Day
8                       Thanksgiving
9                      Christmas Day
10          Christmas Day (Observed)
11         New Year's Day (Observed)
12          Veterans Day (Observed)
13     Independence Day (Observed)
dtype: object
```

Figure 5.3 – US holidays

Each of these holidays has been included in the forecast DataFrame that was covered
in *Chapter 2, Getting Started with Facebook Prophet*. For each holiday, three new columns
are added for the predicted effect of that holiday as well as lower and upper bounds for
the uncertainty, for example, "New Year's Day", "New Year's Day_lower",
and "New Year's Day_upper". Using these new columns, we can see precisely what
effect each holiday is having on our forecast by printing the first non-zero value for each
holiday in the forecast DataFrame.

To do this, let's create a quick function, called first_non_zero. The function takes a
forecast DataFrame and the name of a holiday; it returns the first value for that holiday
that does not equal zero. Then, we'll use a Python list comprehension to loop over each
holiday name and call the first_non_zero function:

```
def first_non_zero(fcst, holiday):
    return fcst[fcst[holiday] != 0][holiday].values[0]


pd.DataFrame({'holiday': model.train_holiday_names,
              'effect': [first_non_zero(forecast, holiday)
                         for holiday in \
                         model.train_holiday_names]})
```

Because each row of the forecast DataFrame is a date, most of the values in each
holiday column will be zero, as the holiday has no effect on these dates. On the date the
holiday occurs, the value will either be positive, indicating more ridership than otherwise
expected, or negative, for less ridership.

Prophet models each holiday as having the same effect every year, so this value will be constant from year to year. Because we set `seasonality_mode='multiplicative'` in this case, these effects are calculated as a percentage deviation from the trend (just to make it clear: the global `seasonality_mode` affects holidays as well). The following table shows these effects:

	holiday	effect
0	New Year's Day	-0.143018
1	Martin Luther King Jr. Day	-0.237753
2	Washington's Birthday	-0.101823
3	Memorial Day	-0.413913
4	Independence Day	-0.554643
5	Labor Day	-0.687805
6	Columbus Day	0.049917
7	Veterans Day	-0.073263
8	Thanksgiving	-0.665720
9	Christmas Day	-0.310232
10	Christmas Day (Observed)	-0.161208
11	New Year's Day (Observed)	-0.128838
12	Veterans Day (Observed)	-0.271374
13	Independence Day (Observed)	-0.158704

Figure 5.4 – Holiday effect values

Now, we can clearly see that `Columbus Day` has a 5% boost to ridership on Divvy. All other holidays have negative effects, with Labor Day having the strongest at 69% fewer riders than the trend would otherwise predict.

This process you've just learned is Prophet's basic holiday functionality; it's analogous to the default seasonalities produced when no additional arguments are provided to Prophet. It works great in many cases and is often all that the model will require. But, just as the analyst can take finer control of seasonality effects, there are several techniques the analyst can use to control holidays beyond the default settings. In the next section, we'll cover the process for adding holidays specific to a state or province.

Adding default state/province holidays

Adding the holidays specific to Illinois is not so straightforward, because the add_
country_holidays method only takes an argument for country, but not state or
province. To add state- or province-level holidays, we need to use a new Prophet function,
make_holidays_df. Let's import it here:

```
from fbprophet.make_holidays import make_holidays_df
```

This function takes as input a list of years for which to populate the holidays as well as
arguments for the country and state or province. Note that you must use all years in
your training DataFrame as well as all years you intend to predict on. That is why, in the
following code, we build a year list to contain all unique years in the training DataFrame.
Then, because our make_future_dataframe command will add one year to the
forecast, we need to extend that year list to include one additional year:

```
year_list = df['ds'].dt.year.unique().tolist()
# Identify the final year, as an integer, and increase it by 1
year_list.append(year_list[-1] + 1)
holidays = make_holidays_df(year_list=year_list,
                            country='US',
                            state='IL')
```

Before moving on, let's take a quick look at the format of this holidays DataFrame by
printing the first five rows:

```
holidays.head()
```

As you can see from the following output, the holidays DataFrame consists of two
columns, ds and holiday, with the date of the holiday and its name, respectively:

	ds	holiday
0	2016-01-01	New Year's Day
1	2016-01-18	Martin Luther King Jr. Day
2	2016-02-12	Lincoln's Birthday
3	2016-02-15	Washington's Birthday
4	2016-03-07	Casimir Pulaski Day

Figure 5.5 – Illinois holidays

To load these holidays into our Prophet model, we simply pass the `holidays` DataFrame to our model when we instantiate it and continue as we have before:

```
model = Prophet(seasonality_mode='multiplicative',
                yearly_seasonality=4,
                holidays=holidays)
model.fit(df)
future = model.make_future_dataframe(periods=365)
forecast = model.predict(future)
```

If you go ahead and call `model.train_holiday_names` again, you will see four additional holidays specific to Illinois that are not official United States holidays: Lincoln's Birthday, Casimir Pulaski Day, Election Day, and Lincoln's Birthday (Observed).

Creating custom holidays

The default holidays for the United States include both Thanksgiving and Christmas, as they are official holidays. However, it's quite plausible that Black Friday and Christmas Eve would also create ridership behavior that deviates from the expected trend. So, we naturally decide to include these in our forecast.

In this example, we will create a DataFrame of the default US holidays in a similar manner to how we created the DataFrame of the Illinois holidays previously, and then add our custom holidays to it. To create custom holidays, you simply need to create a DataFrame with two columns: `holiday` and `ds`. As done previously, it must include all occurrences of the holiday in the past (at least, as far back as your training data goes) and into the future that we intend to forecast.

In this example, we will start by creating the `holidays` DataFrame populated with the default US holidays and use the same `year_list` from the previous example:

```
holidays = make_holidays_df(year_list=year_list,
                            country='US')
```

We are going to enrich this list of default holidays with our custom holidays, so now we will create two DataFrames with the specified columns (`holiday` and `ds`), one for `Black Friday` and one for `Christmas Eve`:

```
black_friday = pd.DataFrame({'holiday': 'Black Friday',
                             'ds': pd.to_datetime(
                                 ['2014-11-28',
```

```
                                '2015-11-27',
                                '2016-11-25',
                                '2017-11-24',
                                '2018-11-23'])})
christmas_eve = pd.DataFrame({'holiday': 'Christmas Eve',
                              'ds': pd.to_datetime(
                              ['2014-12-24',
                                '2015-12-24',
                                '2016-12-24',
                                '2017-12-24',
                                '2018-12-24'])})
```

Of course, you could create just one DataFrame with both holidays as individual rows, but for clarity I have separated them out.

Finally, we just need to concatenate these three holiday DataFrames into just one:

```
holidays = pd.concat([holidays, black_friday,
                      christmas_eve]).sort_values('ds')\
                .reset_index(drop=True)
```

It is not strictly necessary to sort the values or reset the index, as we did in the preceding code, but it does make things a bit clearer if you intend to inspect the DataFrame.

With our holidays DataFrame complete, we now pass it to Prophet when we instantiate the model, just as we did with the Illinois holidays previously, and continue to call fit and predict:

```
model = Prophet(seasonality_mode='multiplicative',
                yearly_seasonality=4,
                holidays=holidays)
model.fit(df)
future = model.make_future_dataframe(periods=365)
forecast = model.predict(future)
```

Now, if you inspect the forecast DataFrame or your components plot, you will indeed see two additional holidays each year, one for Black Friday and one for Thanksgiving.

Creating holidays in this way allows for much more granular control over individual holidays. Next, we'll look at some additional parameters you can use to tune your holidays.

Creating multi-day holidays

Sometimes, a holiday or other special event will span several days. Fortunately, Prophet includes functionality to handle these scenarios via the window arguments. The `holidays` DataFrame we have been building to populate our holidays in the previous examples can have the optional columns of `'lower_window'` and `'upper_window'`. These columns specify additional days either before or after the main holiday that Prophet will model.

For example, in the previous example, we modeled Christmas and Christmas Eve as two different holidays. Another method would have been just to model Christmas but include a `'lower_window'` of 1, telling Prophet to include a single day before Christmas as part of the holiday. This assumes, of course, that Christmas Eve will always fall on the day before Christmas. If, however, Christmas Eve were a holiday that floated and did not always fall immediately before Christmas, this window method would not be used.

Every July, Chicago holds a five-day festival called the *Taste of Chicago*. It is the largest food festival in the world and Chicago's largest festival of any kind. More than one million people attend each year to try food from nearly 100 different vendors or attend popular concerts each day. With such large crowds of people moving around the city, it would be surprising if it had no effect at all on Divvy's ridership. In this example, we will model Taste of Chicago as a 5-day holiday and see what effect that has on Divvy's forecast.

As done previously, we begin by creating the `holidays` DataFrame with the default US holidays. Next, we create a `taste_of_chicago` DataFrame with the dates set as the first day of the event each year of both our historical data and our forecast period. Deviating from the previous example, though, we also include the `'lower_window'` and `'upper_window'` columns, setting the lower to 0 (so we include no dates prior to the first day of the event) and the upper to 4 (which includes four days after the first day of the event, for a total of five days). Then, we concatenate the DataFrames together as follows:

```
holidays = make_holidays_df(year_list=year_list,
                            country='US')


taste_of_chicago = \
pd.DataFrame({'holiday':'Taste of Chicago',
              'ds': pd.to_datetime(['2014-07-09',
                                    '2015-07-08',
                                    '2016-07-06',
                                    '2017-07-05',
                                    '2018-07-11']),
```

```
                  'lower_window': 0,
                  'upper_window': 4})
holidays = pd.concat([holidays, taste_of_chicago])\
                  .sort_values('ds')\
                  .reset_index(drop=True)
```

Now, let's take a look at the first 10 rows of the DataFrame:

```
holidays.head(10)
```

In the output, we see the additional columns as well as the inclusion of the `Taste of Chicago` holiday:

	ds	holiday	lower_window	upper_window
0	2014-01-01	New Year's Day	NaN	NaN
1	2014-01-20	Martin Luther King Jr. Day	NaN	NaN
2	2014-02-17	Washington's Birthday	NaN	NaN
3	2014-05-26	Memorial Day	NaN	NaN
4	2014-07-04	Independence Day	NaN	NaN
5	2014-07-09	Taste of Chicago	0.0	4.0
6	2014-09-01	Labor Day	NaN	NaN
7	2014-10-13	Columbus Day	NaN	NaN
8	2014-11-11	Veterans Day	NaN	NaN
9	2014-11-27	Thanksgiving	NaN	NaN

Figure 5.6 – Holidays with windows

If you're not familiar with the NaN in the preceding table, it stands for *Not a Number*. It's simply a placeholder in this case and has no effect.

And now, we proceed with fitting our model:

```
model = Prophet(seasonality_mode='multiplicative',
                yearly_seasonality=4,
                holidays=holidays)
model.fit(df)
future = model.make_future_dataframe(periods=365)
forecast = model.predict(future)
```

To see what effect `Taste of Chicago` has had on Divvy ridership, let's take a look at the `forecast` DataFrame with this `print` statement:

```
print(forecast[forecast['ds'].isin(['2018-07-11',
                                    '2018-07-12',
                                    '2018-07-13',
                                    '2018-07-14',
                                    '2018-07-15']
)][['ds',
    'Taste of Chicago']])
```

The output is the contents of the `forecast` DataFrame but limited to just the five days of the 2018 event, and the columns for date and the effect of `Taste of Chicago` on ridership:

	ds	Taste of Chicago
1649	2018-07-11	-0.036428
1650	2018-07-12	0.019484
1651	2018-07-13	0.068816
1652	2018-07-14	0.015031
1653	2018-07-15	0.021815

Figure 5.7 – Taste of Chicago effect values

We can see that the first day of the event had 3.6% fewer rides than would have been expected without the event, the second day had 1.9% more rides, and the third 6.8% more. The final two days both had about 2% more rides. The magnitudes of these numbers may not be as large as you had expected, especially with the 4th of July causing a 55% reduction in ridership. And especially when taking into account that one of them is negative and the others positive, it's possible that this result is not a meaningful signal but instead just due to random noise. In *Chapter 10, Uncertainty Intervals*, you will learn how to be certain if this is a meaningful result or not.

We can, however, visualize just this one holiday effect with the new `plot_forecast_ component` function from Prophet's `plot` package. We need to import it first:

```
from fbprophet.plot import plot_forecast_component
```

The function requires the first argument to be the model, the second argument to be the `forecast` DataFrame, and the third argument to be a string naming the component to plot; here we will use `'Taste of Chicago'`:

```
fig3 = plot_forecast_component(model,
                               forecast,
                               'Taste of Chicago',
                               figsize=(10.5, 3.25))
plt.show()
```

In the output, we can visualize exactly what the table in *Figure 5.7* displayed:

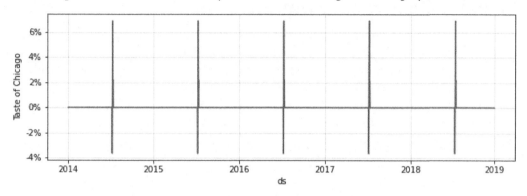

Figure 5.8 – Taste of Chicago holiday effects

The first day of the event shows reduced ridership, and the following four days show increased ridership. Now that we have learned the various ways you can add holidays to your forecasts, let's look at one more tool for controlling holiday effects: regularization.

Regularizing holidays

The process of constraining a model's flexibility to help it generalize better to new data is called **regularization**. *Chapter 4, Seasonality,* featured a lengthy discussion about regularizing the effect of seasonalities in Prophet. The mathematical procedure under Prophet's hood is the same when regularizing both holiday and seasonality effects, so we can use the same concepts from the seasonality chapter and apply them to holidays.

In general, if you as the analyst find that your holidays have more control over your model than you expected, if their absolute magnitudes are higher than you believe is accurate or necessary to model your problem, then you'll want to consider regularization. Regularization will simply compress the magnitude of your holiday effects and forbid them from having as large an effect as they would otherwise. Prophet contains a `holidays_prior_scale` parameter to control this.

This is the same theory behind the `seasonality_prior_scale` parameter that we used in the previous chapter to regularize our seasonalities. Just as seasonalities can be regularized globally or locally, so can holidays. Let's see how to do it next.

Global holiday regularization

Prophet essentially has a default prior probability distribution of guesses for what effect a holiday may have and it uses this distribution to try to find the value that best fits the data. If that prior range of guesses is very far from reality, though, Prophet will struggle to find the best value. You can help it out a lot by giving it additional information about what values to expect, so that it may update its prior distribution to better inform its guesses. Modifying the prior scale for holidays is how you provide this additional information to Prophet.

The values for `holidays_prior_scale` unfortunately don't make much intuitive sense. They are similar to the regularization parameter in lasso regression in that they control the amount of shrinkage. However, you just need to remember that smaller values mean less flexibility—the holiday effect will be dampened through more regularization. By default, Prophet sets this value to 10. Reasonable values range from 10 down to 0.001 or so.

However, every dataset is different, so you'll find experimentation will help a lot. But just like the prior scales for seasonality, you'll find that in most cases a holiday prior scale between 10 and 0.01 will work out well. To see the effect of this variable, let's build one model using the default value of 10 and another model with a much smaller value of 0.05.

Let's also use the `plot_forecast_component` function we learned when plotting the `Taste of Chicago` event, but this time pass the `'holidays'` component to it, to plot all combined holiday effects together. But first, we build the model with the default prior scale value (here, we explicitly set it to `10` for clarity's sake) and then plot only the holiday component to see the holiday effect:

```
model = Prophet(seasonality_mode='multiplicative',
                yearly_seasonality=4,
                holidays_prior_scale=10)
```

```
model.add_country_holidays(country_name='US')
model.fit(df)
future = model.make_future_dataframe(periods=365)
forecast = model.predict(future)
fig = plot_forecast_component(model, forecast, 'holidays')
plt.show()
```

The output of that code will be just the holidays component:

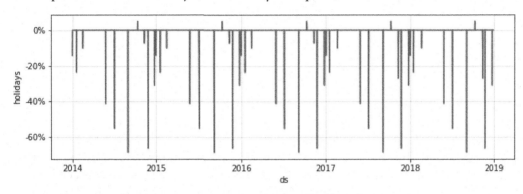

Figure 5.9 – Holidays component with no regularization

With no regularization, Thanksgiving (which we discovered earlier in this chapter to have the strongest effect of all holidays) reduces ridership by about 65%.

Now let's build another model, the same in every way except with strong regularization, and plot the holiday component:

```
model = Prophet(seasonality_mode='multiplicative',
                yearly_seasonality=4,
                holidays_prior_scale=0.05)
model.add_country_holidays(country_name='US')
model.fit(df)
future = model.make_future_dataframe(periods=365)
forecast = model.predict(future)
fig = plot_forecast_component(model, forecast, 'holidays')
plt.show()
```

Again, we used the `plot_forecast_component` function to show only the holidays component:

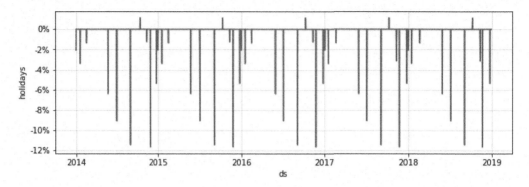

Figure 5.10 – Holidays component with strong regularization

When regularized, the plot appears similar to the plot of unregularized holidays, but with a few differences. First, we see the scale has changed a lot. The strongest holiday effect, when regularized, shows an 11.5% reduction in ridership, compared to the 65% reduction in the unregularized model. The second thing to notice is that all holidays haven't been reduced by an equal proportion: now, it is Christmas that has the strongest effect, not Thanksgiving. This is not an error, just an effect of how regularization works with this many variables interacting with each other.

Choosing a value for the prior scale can be more art than science. You may use your domain knowledge to adjust the value if the holidays' effect seems stronger or weaker than your intuition suggests. If in doubt, experiment and see what works best. The most rigorous approach would be to use grid search with cross-validation, a topic that we will cover near the end of this book.

Using the `holidays_prior_scale` parameter as we did previously adjusts all holidays globally; each holiday across the board is regularized the same amount. For more control, Prophet provides functionality to adjust the prior scale for each individual holiday through the custom holiday interface. In the next example, we'll see just how to do that.

Individual holiday regularization

When adding a new holiday, we created a DataFrame containing two required columns, ds and holiday, and two optional columns, lower_window and upper_window. There is one final optional column we can include in this DataFrame, namely prior_scale. If any holidays have no value in this column (or if the column doesn't even exist in the DataFrame), then the holidays will revert to the global holidays_prior_scale value that we saw in the previous example. In the following example, though, we will add this column and modify some holidays' prior scales individually.

As we have done earlier, we will build the default holiday list and add in some additional holidays. This time around, we will add Black Friday and Christmas Eve with prior scales of 1 and the Taste of Chicago five-day event with a prior scale of 0.1. All other holidays will keep the default prior scale of 10. First, we will use the same year_list created previously to create our holidays DataFrame:

```
holidays = make_holidays_df(year_list=year_list,
                            country='US')
```

This is Prophet's default list of holidays for the US; we want to enrich the list with our three additional holidays. So, now we'll create a DataFrame for each of them. Note that we specify 'prior_scale' for each holiday:

```
black_friday = pd.DataFrame({'holiday': 'Black Friday',
                             'ds': pd.to_datetime(
                                 ['2014-11-28',
                                  '2015-11-27',
                                  '2016-11-25',
                                  '2017-11-24',
                                  '2018-11-23']),
                             'prior_scale': 1})
christmas_eve = pd.DataFrame({'holiday': 'Christmas Eve',
                             'ds': pd.to_datetime(
                                 ['2014-12-24',
                                  '2015-12-24',
                                  '2016-12-24',
                                  '2017-12-24',
                                  '2018-12-24']),
                             'prior_scale': 1})
```

```
taste_of_chicago = \
pd.DataFrame({'holiday': 'Taste of Chicago',
            'ds': pd.to_datetime(['2014-07-09',
                                  '2015-07-08',
                                  '2016-07-06',
                                  '2017-07-05',
                                  '2018-07-11']),
            'lower_window': 0,
            'upper_window': 4,
            'prior_scale': 0.1})
```

The last step is to combine these four DataFrames:

```
holidays = pd.concat([holidays,
                     black_friday,
                     christmas_eve,
                     taste_of_chicago]
                    ).sort_values('ds')\
                     .reset_index(drop=True)
```

In the DataFrames for `Black Friday`, `Christmas Eve`, and `Taste of Chicago`, we added that additional column of `prior_scale`. Let's print the first 16 rows of the `holidays` DataFrame to confirm this:

```
holidays.head(16)
```

As you can see in the following table, we have our 10 default holidays, with no prior scale or windows added. We have the `Taste of Chicago` event with the upper window for four additional days, and a prior scale of `0.1`. Both `Black Friday` and `Christmas Eve` have their prior scales of `1`. Prophet will apply the default prior scale where missing when it builds the model. Remember, NaN, for *Not a Number*, means an empty cell in this case:

	ds	holiday	prior_scale	lower_window	upper_window
0	2014-01-01	New Year's Day	NaN	NaN	NaN
1	2014-01-20	Martin Luther King Jr. Day	NaN	NaN	NaN
2	2014-02-12	Lincoln's Birthday	NaN	NaN	NaN
3	2014-02-17	Washington's Birthday	NaN	NaN	NaN
4	2014-03-03	Casimir Pulaski Day	NaN	NaN	NaN
5	2014-05-26	Memorial Day	NaN	NaN	NaN
6	2014-07-04	Independence Day	NaN	NaN	NaN
7	2014-07-09	Taste of Chicago	0.1	0.0	4.0
8	2014-09-01	Labor Day	NaN	NaN	NaN
9	2014-10-13	Columbus Day	NaN	NaN	NaN
10	2014-11-04	Election Day	NaN	NaN	NaN
11	2014-11-11	Veterans Day	NaN	NaN	NaN
12	2014-11-27	Thanksgiving	NaN	NaN	NaN
13	2014-11-28	Black Friday	1.0	NaN	NaN
14	2014-12-24	Christmas Eve	1.0	NaN	NaN
15	2014-12-25	Christmas Day	NaN	NaN	NaN

Figure 5.11 – Holidays with prior scales

With our `holidays` DataFrame built, we simply continue to instantiate our model, fit, and predict in order to build the forecast:

```
model = Prophet(seasonality_mode='multiplicative',
                yearly_seasonality=4,
                holidays=holidays,
                holidays_prior_scale=10)
model.fit(df)
future = model.make_future_dataframe(periods=365)
forecast = model.predict(future)
```

Now with the `forecast` DataFrame created, you can experiment on your own using the plotting tools you've learned about so far to explore the results.

Choosing an appropriate prior scale, both for holidays and for seasonalities, may sometimes be difficult. Prophet's default values tend to work very well in most cases, but there may be times when you need to change them and struggle to find the best value. In these cases, cross-validation is your best approach. You will learn how to use cross-validation with an appropriate performance metric to optimize your Prophet models in *Chapter 12, Performance Metrics*.

Summary

In this chapter, you first learned how to add the default holidays for a country and then went a bit deeper by adding in any state or province holidays. After that, you learned how to add custom holidays and expanded this technique to adjust for holidays that span multiple days. Finally, you learned what regularization is and how it is used to control overfitting, and how to apply it globally to all holidays in your model or more granularly by specifying different regularization for each individual holiday.

Holidays often cause massive spikes in time series and ignoring their effects will cause Prophet to perform very poorly in its forecast results. The tools in this chapter will allow your models to accommodate these external events and provide a way to predict the effects running into the future.

In the next chapter, we'll look at the different growth modes available in Prophet. So far, all our models have had linear growth but that may not be the only mode you will encounter in your forecasting work!

6
Growth Modes

So far in this book, every forecast we've built followed only one growth mode: **linear**. The trend sometimes had some small bends where the slope either increased or decreased, but fundamentally the trend consisted of linear segments. However, Prophet features two additional growth modes: **logistic** and **flat**.

Modeling your time series with a growth mode that is not optimal can often fit the actual data very well. But, as you'll see in this chapter, even if the fit is realistic, the future forecast can become wildly unrealistic. Sometimes the shape of the data will inform which growth mode to choose and sometimes you'll need domain knowledge and a bit of common sense. This chapter will help guide you to an appropriate selection. Furthermore, you will learn when and how to apply these different growth modes. Specifically, this chapter will cover the following:

- Applying linear growth
- Understanding the logistic function
- Saturating forecasts
- Applying flat growth

Technical requirements

The data files and code for examples in this chapter can be found at `https://github.com/PacktPublishing/Forecasting-Time-Series-Data-with-Facebook-Prophet`.

Applying linear growth

All the models we built in the previous chapters had the default growth mode, linear. This means that the trend consists of a straight, sloped line, or potentially a few straight, sloped lines connected at changepoints, a case we will explore in *Chapter 7, Trend Changepoints*. For now, though, let's load up our Divvy data again and focus on the growth.

We're going to import `pandas`, `matplotlib`, and `Prophet` again, but this time we'll also import a new function from Prophet's `plot` package, `add_changepoints_to_plot`, as follows:

```
import pandas as pd
import matplotlib.pyplot as plt
from fbprophet import Prophet
from fbprophet.plot import add_changepoints_to_plot
```

This new function will allow us to easily plot our trend line directly on our forecast plot.

As we've done previously, let's open the Divvy data and load it into our training DataFrame:

```
df = pd.read_csv('divvy_daily.csv')
df = df[['date', 'rides']]
df['date'] = pd.to_datetime(df['date'])
df.columns = ['ds', 'y']
```

We learned already in *Chapter 4, Seasonality*, that this dataset should be modeled with multiplicative seasonality and that the yearly seasonality should be constrained a bit by setting the Fourier order to 4. We'll set these values when instantiating our model. We'll also explicitly set `growth='linear'`. This is the default, and previously we just implicitly accepted it, but for clarity's sake we'll include it here:

```
model = Prophet(growth='linear',
                seasonality_mode='multiplicative',
                yearly_seasonality=4)
```

Just as we did when we modeled the daily Divvy data in the seasonality chapter, we will next fit the model, build a `future` DataFrame with one year to forecast, predict future values, and plot the forecast. This time, however, we will use the `add_changepoints_to_plot` function.

The function requires that we specify which plot axes to use, identify the model we created, and identify the forecast DataFrame output from the `predict` method. For the axes, we use the Matplotlib `gca` method, for *get current axes*, and call it on the figure created when plotting the forecast. You can see the syntax in the following code. We are only using the plot changepoints function here to plot the trend so we will remove the changepoint markers for now using `cp_linestyle=''`:

```
model.fit(df)
future = model.make_future_dataframe(periods=365)
forecast = model.predict(future)
fig = model.plot(forecast)
add_changepoints_to_plot(fig.gca(), model, forecast,
                         cp_linestyle='')
plt.show()
```

As output, you should now see a similar forecast to that from *Figure 4.8*, but this time the trend line will be overlaid upon the plot:

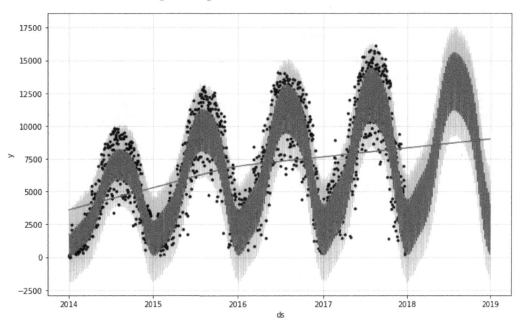

Figure 6.1 – Divvy forecast with trend

Remember, Prophet is an additive regression model. So, the trend is the most fundamental building block of our forecast. We add detail and variation to it by adding seasonalities, holidays, and additional regressors. The trend you see in the preceding figure (the solid line cutting through the midpoints of each sine period) is the Divvy plot with seasonality removed (we never added holidays in this example).

As you can see, the trend is a straight segment from **2014** until late **2016**, then a slight bend and another straight segment, with a shallower slope, from **2016** onward. Despite that bend, it is fundamentally linear.

Let's now look at the next growth mode, logistic. To understand this growth mode, you first need to understand the logistic function.

Understanding the logistic function

The **logistic function** generates an S-shaped curve; the equation takes the following form:

$$y = \frac{L}{1 + e^{-k(x-x_0)}}$$

Figure 6.2 – The logistic function

Here, L is the maximum value of the curve, k is the logistic growth rate, or steepness, of the curve, and $x0$ is the x-value of the curve's midpoint.

Taking $L = 1$, $k = 1$, and $x_0 = 0$, the logistic function produces the **standard logistic function**, seen in the following plot:

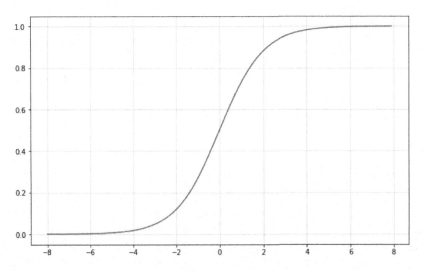

Figure 6.3 – The standard logistic function, y = 1 / (1 + e-x)

If you have studied logistic regression or neural networks, you may recognize this as the **sigmoid function**. Any input value for x, from $-\infty$ to ∞, will be squished into an output value, y, between 0 and 1. This equation is what allows a logistic regression model to accept any input value and output a probability between 0 and 1.

The equation was developed by Pierre François Verhulst, a Belgian mathematician, in a series of three papers published between 1838 and 1847. Verhulst was working to model the population growth of Belgium.

Population growth approximately follows an initial exponential growth rate, then a linear, also known as arithmetic, growth rate, until the population hits a saturation point, where growth slows to zero. This is the shape you see in the preceding plot, starting at the curve's midpoint and moving right. Verhulst invented the term *logistic* to be analogous to *arithmetic* and *geometric* but derived from *logarithmic*. Don't get the word confused with *logistics*, as referring to the handling of details. They have completely different origins.

Prophet's logistic growth mode follows this general curve. The curve's **saturation** levels are the upper and lower bounds, which the curve asymptotically approaches.

Besides applications in statistics and machine learning, where the logistic curve is used in logistic regression and neural networks, the logistic function is also often used to model population growth, either of humans as in Verhulst's Belgium or of animals as we will do in this chapter. It is used often in medicine to model the growth of tumors, bacterial or viral loads in an infected person, or infection rates of people during a pandemic.

In economics and sociology, the curve is used to describe the adoption rate of new innovations. Linguists use it to model language changes. It can even be used to model the spread of a rumor or new idea throughout a population.

Let's see how to apply this in Prophet.

Saturating forecasts

In the early 1800s, westward expansion in the United States brought many settlers and their livestock into contact with the native wolf population. These wolves began to prey on the domestic stock, which resulted in the settlers hunting and killing the wolves in order to protect their own animals. The gray wolf was still present on the land which became Yellowstone National Park when it was established in 1872, but over the next few decades they were hunted nearly to extinction in the region and throughout the lower 48 states.

In the 1960s, the public began to understand the idea of ecosystems and the interconnectedness of species, and in 1975, the decision to restore wolf populations to Yellowstone was taken, with 31 gray wolves finally being relocated to the park from Canada in 1995. This provided an almost perfect experiment of natural population growth inside the park.

We'll look at this population in the next few examples. However, we'll be using simulated data because the true data is spotty throughout the historical record. As the wolves tend to avoid human contact, counting their number can never be exact and so accurate data is lacking. Furthermore, there are numerous compounding factors that we will not model (and are generally unpredictable, as well).

To understand these compounding factors, consider the example of Isle Royale, an island on Michigan's Lake Superior that has had a moose and wolf population under continuous study since 1959. This is, in fact, the longest continuous study of any predator-prey population system in the world. As can be seen in the following plot, it has not been a predictable system, to say the least:

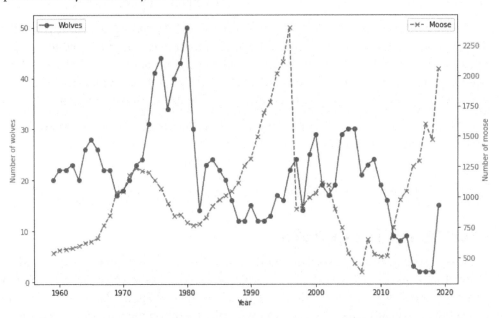

Figure 6.4 – Population numbers of wolves and moose on Isle Royale

In the 1960s and 1970s, rising moose populations provided food, which allowed wolf populations to double. But in 1980, humans inadvertently introduced canine-parvovirus, a disease that caused the wolf population to collapse. The moose population in turn rose again with the decline of its only predator, only to collapse itself in 1996 with the double stresses of the most severe winter on record and an unpredictable outbreak of moose ticks.

Throughout the 1990s, the wolf population was too low for healthy breeding, leading to intense levels of inbreeding, which held their population down, only rebounding when a single wolf reached the island by crossing winter ice from Canada in the late 1990s. Following this, the wolf population increased throughout the early twenty-first century, despite declining moose numbers. All this is to say that small, isolated populations represent a very dynamic system that cannot be accurately predicted when not in isolation from natural external events.

Increasing logistic growth

To synthesize a somewhat realistic population of wolves in Yellowstone, let's suppose that 100 wolves were introduced in 1995. Park ecologists surveyed the area and determined that the land could support a total population of 500 wolves.

In the linear growth example, we imported `pandas`, `matplotlib`, `Prophet`, and the `add_changepoints_to_plot` function, so to continue we only need to import the `numpy` and `random` libraries in order to create our dataset. Be sure to set the random seed so that every time we run the code we get the same pseudo-random results:

```
import numpy as np
import random
random.seed(42)   # set random seed for repeatability
```

We will simulate the wolf population by first creating a series of monthly dates, from 1995 until 2004. At every date, we'll calculate the output from our logistic equation. Then, we'll add some sinusoidal variation to account for yearly seasonality, and finally some random noise. Then, we just need to scale our curve up:

```
x = pd.to_datetime(pd.date_range('1995-01', '2004-02',
                         freq='M')\
                .strftime("%Y-%b").tolist())
y = [1 / (1 + np.e ** (-.03 * (val - 50))) for val in \
        range(len(x))]   # create logistic curve
# add sinusoidal variation
y = [y[idx] + y[idx] * .01 * np.sin((idx - 2) * (360 / 12)\
        * (np.pi / 180)) for idx in range(len(y))]
# add noise
y = [val + random.uniform(-.01, .01) for val in y]
y = [int(500 * val) for val in y]   # scale up
```

Let's plot the curve to make sure everything worked out as expected:

```
plt.figure(figsize=(10, 6))
plt.plot(x, y)
plt.show()
```

If everything went correctly, you should see this plot:

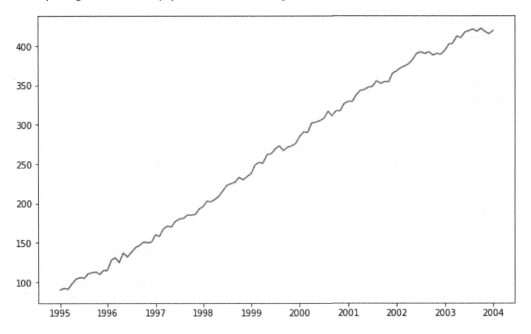

Figure 6.5 – Simulated wolf population in Yellowstone

Let's begin our analysis of this data by fitting a Prophet model with linear growth. This example will demonstrate what can go wrong when choosing an inappropriate growth mode.

Modeling with linear growth

As we did earlier, we start by organizing our data into a DataFrame for Prophet:

```
df = pd.DataFrame({'ds': pd.to_datetime(x), 'y': y})
```

In addition to linear growth, let's set the Fourier order of the yearly seasonality to 3 and the seasonality mode to `multiplicative`. Then, we fit our DataFrame and create the `future` DataFrame. We simulated this data at a monthly frequency, so we'll forecast out 10 years and set `freq='M'`. After predicting on the future, we'll plot the forecast and use the `add_changepoints_to_plot` function to overlay the trend:

```
model = Prophet(growth='linear',
                yearly_seasonality=3,
                seasonality_mode='multiplicative')
model.fit(df)
future = model.make_future_dataframe(periods=12 * 10,
                                     freq='M')
forecast = model.predict(future)
fig = model.plot(forecast)
add_changepoints_to_plot(fig.gca(), model, forecast,
                         cp_linestyle='')
plt.show()
```

Immediately, you should see what will go wrong with using a linear trend in a situation where the forecast will naturally saturate at some level. The predicted values will keep rising toward infinity with longer and longer forecast time periods:

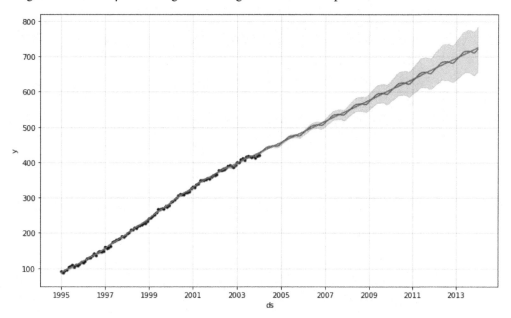

Figure 6.6 – Wolf population forecast with linear growth

Obviously, this cannot be realistic. There is only so much food for the wolves to eat; at a certain point, there won't be enough food and the wolves will begin starving. Let's now model this with logistic growth and see what happens.

Modeling with logistic growth

With **logistic** growth, Prophet always requires that a **ceiling** be stated—a value that your forecast will not ever surpass. In cases where growth is declining, a floor must be stated as well. In this example, though, we have increasing growth, so we'll only set the ceiling. Prophet refers to it as a **cap**. To add this to Prophet, we need to create a new column in our training DataFrame called cap and also mimic it in our future DataFrame.

In general, determining a cap may pose some difficulties. If your curve is near the saturation level already, you can see better what value it is approaching and choose it. If not, however, then a little domain knowledge will really be your best solution. Before you can model logistic growth rates, you must have some idea of where the saturation level will eventually be. Usually, this cap is set using data or with special expertise about market size. For our example, we'll set the cap to 500, as that was the value estimated by the ecologists:

```
df['cap'] = 500
```

Next, we continue just as we did in the previous example, but this time let's set the growth mode to logistic, before fitting and creating the future DataFrame:

```
model = Prophet(growth='logistic',
                yearly_seasonality=3,
                seasonality_mode='multiplicative')
model.fit(df)
future = model.make_future_dataframe(periods=12 * 10,
                                     freq='M')
```

We need to add the cap to our future DataFrame as well:

```
future['cap'] = 500
```

Now when we predict and plot the forecast, you'll see quite a differently shaped curve:

```
forecast = model.predict(future)
fig = model.plot(forecast)
add_changepoints_to_plot(fig.gca(), model, forecast,
                         cp_linestyle='')
plt.show()
```

By default, Prophet displays the cap, and floor if present, as horizontal dashed lines in your plot:

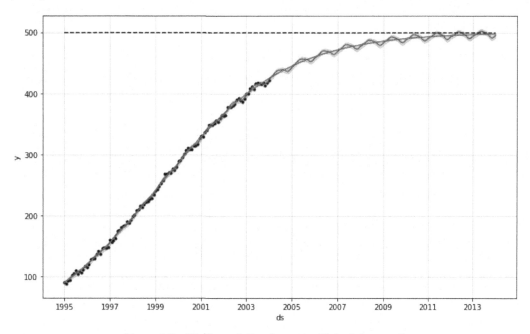

Figure 6.7 – Wolf population forecast with logistic growth

With logistic growth, the wolf population is allowed to grow at roughly the same rate for several years. The growth rate slows as it approaches its saturation point, the greatest population that the natural resources available can support. After this point, the growth rate stays flat with just a bit of seasonal variation as old wolves die in the winter and spring pups arrive.

Non-constant cap

It is important to note that the cap does not necessarily need to be constant. If you are forecasting sales, for example, your saturation limit will be the market size. But this market size may be growing as various factors cause more consumers to consider purchasing your product. Let's look at a quick example of how to model this. We assumed that the wolf population in Yellowstone was constrained by the size of the park. Let's now create a hypothetical situation where the park size is gradually increased starting in 2007, creating conditions that allow for two additional wolves per month.

Let's create a function to set the cap. For dates prior to 2007, we will keep the park's saturation limit of 500. For all dates starting in 2007, though, we will increase the cap by two per month:

```python
def set_cap(row, df):
    if row.year < 2007:
        return 500
    else:
        pop_2007 = 500
        idx_2007 = df[df['ds'].dt.year == 2007].index[0]
        idx_date = df[df['ds'] == row].index[0]
        return pop_2007 + 2 * (idx_date - idx_2007)
```

Now, let's set the cap for our training DataFrame, df:

```python
df['cap'] = df['ds'].apply(set_cap, args=(df,))
```

The cap should remain 500 throughout, as our training data ends in 2004. Now, let's create our model the same as before, but set our future DataFrame using the set_cap function:

```python
model = Prophet(growth='logistic',
                yearly_seasonality=3,
                seasonality_mode='multiplicative')
model.fit(df)
future = model.make_future_dataframe(periods=12 * 10,
                                     freq='M')
future['cap'] = future['ds'].apply(set_cap, args=(future,))
forecast = model.predict(future)
fig = model.plot(forecast)
add_changepoints_to_plot(fig.gca(), model, forecast,
```

```
                          cp_linestyle='')
plt.show()
```

Now, you can see that the wolf population is asymptotically approaching our increasing cap:

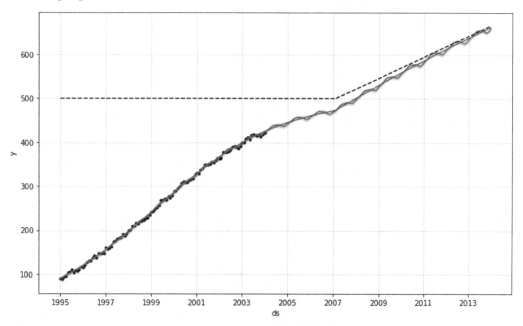

Figure 6.8 – Wolf population forecast with non-constant cap

The cap is simply a value set for each row in the DataFrame; for every date, you can set whichever value makes sense. The cap may be constant as in our first example, or it may vary linearly, as we have just done here, or it may follow any arbitrary curve of your choosing.

Now let's look at the reverse situation, a hypothetical situation where the wolf population is sadly declining and approaching extinction.

Decreasing logistic growth

The only difference in this example is that we must also state a `floor` value in addition to a `cap` value. Let's build another psuedo-random dataset but with negative growth:

```
x = pd.to_datetime(pd.date_range('1995-01','2035-02',
                                 freq='M')\
                   .strftime("%Y-%b").tolist())
```

```
y = [1 - 1 / (1 + np.e ** (-.03 * (val - 50))) for val in \
    range(len(x))]   # create logistic curve
# add sinusoidal variation
y = [y[idx] + y[idx] * .05 * np.sin((idx - 2) * (360 / 12)\
    * (np.pi / 180)) for idx in range(len(y))]
# add noise
y = [val + 5 * val * random.uniform(-.01, .01) for val \
    in y]
y = [int(500 * val) for val in y]   # scale up
plt.figure(figsize=(10, 6))
plt.plot(x, y)
plt.show()
```

The growth curve should look like this:

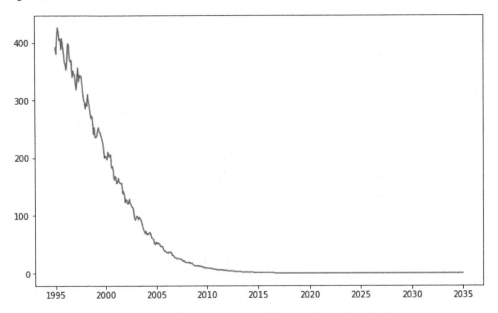

Figure 6.9 – Simulated declining wolf population in Yellowstone

For our forecast in this case, we'll cut off the data at 2006 and attempt to predict when there will be no more wolves in the population. When creating our DataFrame, we specify both a cap value, as we did previously, and a floor value:

```
df2 = pd.DataFrame({'ds': pd.to_datetime(x), 'y': y})
df2 = df2[df2['ds'].dt.year < 2006]
```

```
df2['cap'] = 500
df2['floor'] = 0
```

We'll complete the model all in one step. Everything is the same as before, except this time we also set `floor` in the `future` DataFrame:

```
model = Prophet(growth='logistic',
                yearly_seasonality=3,
                seasonality_mode='multiplicative')
model.fit(df2)
future = model.make_future_dataframe(periods=12 * 10,
                                     freq='M')
future['cap'] = 500
future['floor'] = 0
forecast = model.predict(future)
fig = model.plot(forecast)
add_changepoints_to_plot(fig.gca(), model, forecast,
                         cp_linestyle='')
plt.show()
```

It should come as no surprise that Prophet handles this case with ease:

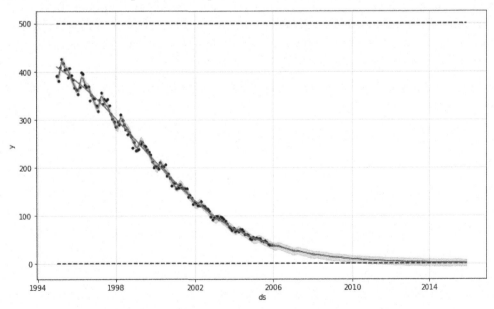

Figure 6.10 – Wolf population forecast with decreasing logistic growth

Prophet will predict precise decimal values and of course wolves exist in integer values, but this plot shows that somewhere between 2010 and 2014, the wolf population will die off. In a real scenario, it also matters greatly whether the last few remaining wolves are part of a breeding pair, and we have ignored that factor here.

Notice that because we have specified both a cap and a floor, Prophet has plotted both as horizontal dashed lines. When logistic growth is declining, even if there is no relevant cap, as is the case here, one must be included in your model. You may choose one that is arbitrarily high with no effect on your model, although be aware that it will be included in your plot and may make it appear as if Prophet's forecast is very low.

You can, however, exclude it from your plots by including the `plot_cap` argument as done here: `fig = model.plot(forecast, plot_cap=False)`, which modifies both the cap and the floor. Prophet does not currently support the exclusion of only one of these from your plot.

Prophet currently supports one more growth mode: no growth. However, the Prophet team is at work on some other modes at the time of writing and those may become available soon, so keep an eye on the documentation. Let's take a look at this final growth mode.

Applying flat growth

Flat growth is when the trend line is perfectly constant throughout the data. The data's values only differ due to seasonality, holidays, extra regressors, or noise. To see how to model flat growth, let's continue on with our wolf population but this time consider far into the future when the population has fully stabilized.

Let's begin by creating a new dataset, essentially the same as our logistic growth dataset but with a much longer timeframe:

```
x = pd.to_datetime(pd.date_range('1995-01','2096-02',
                             freq='M')\
                .strftime("%Y-%b").tolist())
# create logistic curve

y = [1 / (1 + np.e ** (-.03 * (val - 50))) for val in \
        range(len(x))]
  # add sinusoidal variation
y = [y[idx] + y[idx] * .01 * np.sin((idx - 2) * (360 / 12)\
        * (np.pi / 180)) for idx in range(len(y))]
```

```
# add noise
y = [val + 1 * val * random.uniform(-.01, .01) for val \
     in y]
y = [int(500 * val) for val in y]    # scale up
plt.figure(figsize=(10, 6))
plt.plot(x, y)
plt.show()
```

We are now looking forward a century from when the wolves were re-introduced into the park:

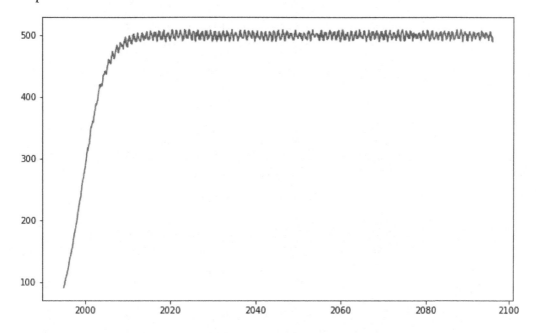

Figure 6.11 – Simulated wolf population over a century

After this length of time, the wolf population has reached the saturation point and is fully stabilized. We will now create our training DataFrame, but then only limit our data to the last decade of the range, where the overall trend is already well saturated:

```
df = pd.DataFrame({'ds': pd.to_datetime(x), 'y': y})
df = df[df['ds'].dt.year > 2085]
plt.figure(figsize=(10, 6))
plt.plot(df['ds'], df['y'])
plt.show()
```

Plotting that data should show no overall growth, just very noisy seasonality:

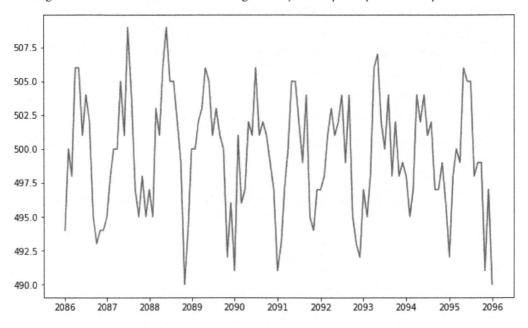

Figure 6.12 – Simulated stable wolf population

Let's first use the default linear growth to see what could go wrong:

```
model = Prophet(growth='linear',
                yearly_seasonality=3,
                seasonality_mode='multiplicative')
model.fit(df)
future = model.make_future_dataframe(periods=12 * 10,
                                     freq='M')
forecast = model.predict(future)
fig = model.plot(forecast)
add_changepoints_to_plot(fig.gca(), model, forecast,
                         cp_linestyle='')
plt.show()
```

Due to random noise in the data, Prophet will find brief areas where there seems to be a trend, either positive or negative. If one of these periods occurs at the end of the training data, then that curve will continue for the entire output of forecasted future data:

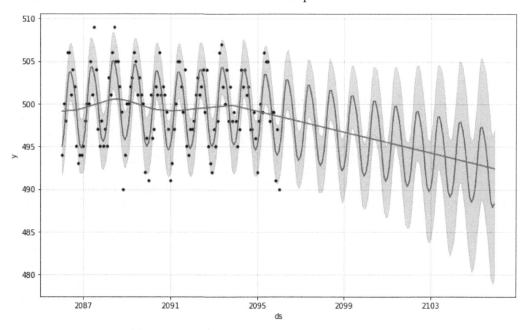

Figure 6.13 – Stable wolf population forecast with linear growth

As you can see, Prophet predicts that the wolf population is decreasing even though it is quite stable. Furthermore, the uncertainty intervals are growing; Prophet is smart enough to know this isn't quite right. Now let's model this correctly—with flat growth. Because the trend will be constant, setting a seasonality mode is irrelevant. It will still be calculated as either additive or multiplicative, but the end result will be the same in either case. We will ignore it here.

Creating a model with flat growth is as simple as setting `growth='flat'` during model instantiation:

```
model = Prophet(growth='flat',
                yearly_seasonality=3)
model.fit(df)
future = model.make_future_dataframe(periods=12 * 10,
                                     freq='M')
forecast = model.predict(future)
fig = model.plot(forecast)
```

```
add_changepoints_to_plot(fig.gca(), model, forecast,
                         cp_linestyle='')
plt.show()
```

Now, Prophet's trend line is perfectly flat:

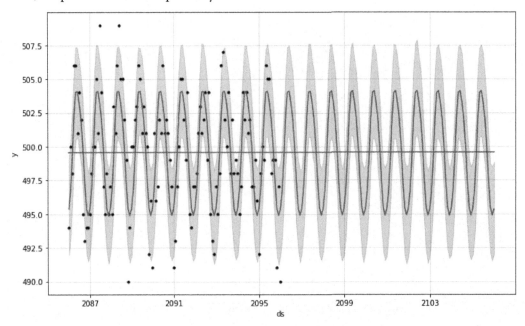

Figure 6.14 – Stable wolf population forecast with flat growth

No matter how far out we forecast, the trend will be stable. The only variation in Prophet's model in this example comes from the yearly seasonality as we added no holidays and neither daily nor weekly seasonalities were included.

Summary

In this chapter, you learned that the models we built in the first few chapters of this book all featured linear growth. You learned that the logistic function was developed to model population growth and then learned how to implement this in Prophet by modeling the growth of the wolf population in Yellowstone after their reintroduction in 1995.

Logistic growth in Prophet can be modeled as either increasing up to a saturation limit called the *cap* or decreasing to a saturation limit called the *floor*. Finally, you learned how to model flat (or no growth) trends, where the trend is fixed to one value for the entire data period but seasonality is still allowed to vary. Throughout this chapter, you used the `add_changepoints_to_plot` function in order to overlay the trend line on your forecast plots.

Choosing the correct growth mode is important, and particularly so when forecasting further into the future. We looked at a couple of examples in this chapter where the incorrect growth mode fitted the actual data well, but the future forecasts became quite unrealistic. In the next chapter, you'll learn all about changepoints and how to use them to gain even more control over your trend lines.

7
Trend Changepoints

During the development of Prophet, the engineering team recognized that real-world time series will frequently exhibit abrupt changes in their trajectories. As a fundamentally linear regression model, Prophet would not be capable of capturing these changes without special care being taken. You may have noticed in the previous chapters, however, that when we plotted the forecast components in our examples, the trend line was not always perfectly straight. Clearly, the Prophet team has developed a way for Prophet to capture these bends in the linear model. The locations of these bends are called **changepoints**.

Prophet will automatically identify these changepoints and allow the trend to adapt appropriately. However, there are several tools you can use to control this behavior if Prophet is underfitting or overfitting these rate changes. In this chapter, we'll look at Prophet's automatic changepoint detection to provide you with an understanding of what is happening in your model with the default settings. We will then look at two further techniques you can use if you need finer control over the changepoint process.

Specifically, in this chapter you will learn about the following:

- Automatic trend changepoint detection
- Regularizing changepoints
- Specifying custom changepoint locations

Technical requirements

The data files and code for examples in this chapter can be found at
`https://github.com/PacktPublishing/Forecasting-Time-Series-Data-with-Facebook-Prophet`.

Automatic trend changepoint detection

Trend changepoints are locations in your time series where the trend component of the model suddenly changes its slope. There could be many reasons why these changepoints occur, depending upon your dataset. For example, Facebook developed Prophet to forecast their own business problems; they may be modeling the number of daily active users and see a sudden change of trend upon the release of a new feature.

Airline passenger numbers may suddenly change as economies of scale allow much cheaper flights. The trend of carbon dioxide in the atmosphere was relatively flat for tens of thousands of years, but then suddenly changed during the Industrial Revolution.

From our work with the Divvy dataset in previous chapters, we saw a slow-down of growth after approximately two years. Let's take a closer look at this example to learn about automatic changepoint detection.

Default changepoint detection

Prophet sets changepoints by first specifying a number of potential dates where a changepoint may occur. Prophet then works on calculating the magnitude of change at each of these points, attempting to fit the trend curve while keeping those magnitudes as low as possible. You can tune Prophet's flexibility here by adjusting `changepoint_prior_scale`. You may recognize that argument from earlier—both seasonalities and holidays had their own prior scales for regularization.

With changepoints, it has much the same effect, and we'll explore it later in this chapter. In Prophet's default settings, the magnitudes of most of these potential changepoints will very nearly be zero and therefore will have a negligible effect on our trend curve.

To get started with our code, we need to make the necessary imports and load our Divvy data. We'll be using the daily Divvy data here. We are also going to import the `add_changepoints_to_plot` function, which you were introduced to in *Chapter 6, Growth Modes*; we'll be using that a lot here:

```
import pandas as pd
import matplotlib.pyplot as plt
from fbprophet import Prophet
```

```
from fbprophet.plot import add_changepoints_to_plot

df = pd.read_csv('divvy_daily.csv')
df = df[['date', 'rides']]
df['date'] = pd.to_datetime(df['date'])
df.columns = ['ds', 'y']
```

With the default settings, Prophet will place 25 potential changepoints, evenly spaced in the first 80% of the data, before determining their magnitudes. With this Divvy data, those 25 locations are denoted by the vertical dashed bars in this image:

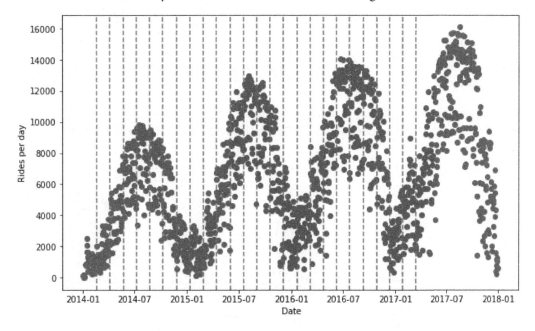

Figure 7.1 – Divvy data with potential changepoint locations

Now, let's fit our Prophet model. In this step, Prophet will determine what magnitudes to apply at each of those potential changepoints. From examples in the previous chapters, we've learned how to model this data with multiplicative seasonality and to hold down the Fourier order of the yearly seasonality a bit. You can see that reflected here when we instantiate our Prophet object.

After fitting the model, we'll call `predict` with no `future` DataFrame specified, which causes Prophet to build its model and predict historical values but not any forecasted ones:

```
model = Prophet(seasonality_mode='multiplicative',
                yearly_seasonality=4)
```

```
model.fit(df)
forecast = model.predict()
```

At this point, we will plot the model. We use the `add_changepoints_to_plot` function to see the locations of significant changepoints. As you saw in *Chapter 6, Growth Modes*, the `add_changepoints_to_plot` function takes three required arguments. The first argument is the axes upon which to add the changepoints. We specify `fig` created in our first plot call, with the `gca()` method, which stands for *get current axes*. The second argument is our model and the third argument is our forecast.

In *Chapter 6, Growth Modes*, we used the `cp_linestyle` argument to force Prophet not to plot the changepoints but only the trend; we will not use that argument in this case:

```
fig = model.plot(forecast)
add_changepoints_to_plot(fig.gca(), model, forecast)
plt.show()
```

You should now see that Prophet determined that 5 of those 25 potential changepoints are actually significant. These five are denoted with the vertical dashed lines in this plot:

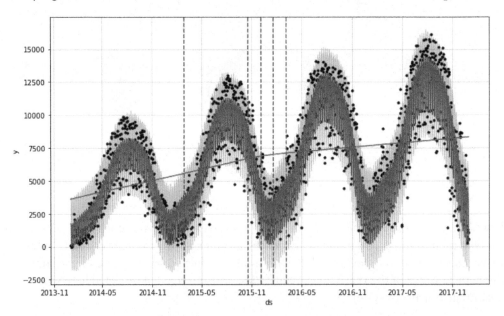

Figure 7.2 – Divvy changepoint plot

It is hard to tell with the first changepoint that the trend is actually bending, but with the next four it is much clearer. At each of those changepoints, the slope of the trend is allowed to become shallower.

The magnitude of each of the 25 potential changepoints is stored in `model.params`, but these values have been normalized so their absolute values are meaningless but their relative magnitudes are not. The model parameters are stored in a dictionary, with `'delta'` being the key for the changepoint magnitudes. Let's take a look:

```
print(model.params['delta'])
```

In this model, those changepoint magnitudes should be similar to the changepoint magnitudes shown in *Figure 7.3*. Because these numbers are calculated through an optimization process instead of a deterministic equation, you may arrive at different exact values but the exponents should be roughly the same:

```
[[-1.79323684e-08 -1.60747569e-07 -2.72344253e-03 -4.29119902e-03
  -5.74359502e-08 -1.95943493e-08  2.39423581e-08  3.99224400e-08
   3.08280300e-02  1.58073660e-07 -2.04451104e-08  2.28463921e-09
  -6.70654988e-03 -9.56743518e-02 -8.63950281e-02 -5.48295844e-02
  -3.19821946e-02 -1.24969134e-05 -2.17687237e-05 -2.32544199e-09
  -9.75395931e-09 -2.26544119e-08 -5.42697251e-08 -8.86291306e-09
  -6.77990839e-08]]
```

Figure 7.3 – Divvy changepoint magnitudes

Most of those magnitudes have an exponent of -08 or -09, meaning that in standard notation you should shift the decimal point that number of digits eight or nine digits to the left, which is to say that those numbers are very close to zero. You can visualize these magnitudes by plotting them. Here, I am overlaying the trend line and the significant changepoints with the magnitudes of all changepoints:

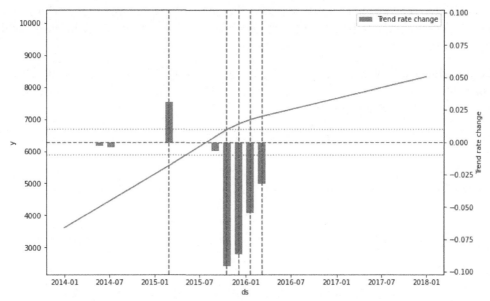

Figure 7.4 – Changepoint magnitudes

Let me explain this plot a bit. The left axis is the same **y** axis as in *Figure 7.2*. The trend line—the solid line cutting from lower left across to upper right—is plotted on this axis. The vertical dashed lines are the significant changepoints identified by Prophet. The solid vertical bars are the changepoint magnitudes; these are plotted on the right axis, **Trend rate change**.

Again, most of these magnitudes are very nearly zero so they do not appear on the plot. The horizontal dashed line denotes a changepoint magnitude of zero. Bars extending upward from here are changepoints with positive magnitude, where the trend bends upward, and bars extending downward from here are changepoints with negative magnitude, where the trend bends downward.

The add_changepoints_to_plot function will *only* plot those changepoints with an absolute magnitude greater than 0.01. The two horizontal dotted lines are located at magnitude levels of 0.01 and -0.01; Prophet only plots magnitudes that extend beyond these limits. You can change this threshold using the threshold argument in the function; for example, add_changepoints_to_plot(fig.gca(), model, forecast, threshold=0.1) will widen that threshold to an upper bound of 0.1 and a lower bound of -0.1. This only affects the plotting visualization, not your actual changepoints.

So, *Figure 7.4* illustrates that Prophet was successful in forcing nearly all of the potential changepoints to have an insignificant effect. Eight total changepoints had magnitudes large enough to be visible on our plot, but only five of them were higher than Prophet's plotting threshold (although their small effect on the trend is still applied). Even though it can be hard to see, the only positively valued changepoint, plotted just after 2015-01, does indeed cause the trend to bend a little bit more steeply at that point. At the locations of the other significant changepoints, the trend becomes shallower.

The preceding example demonstrates Prophet's behavior with regard to changepoints in a fully automatic setting. In the next section, let's examine the levers you can use to gain some control of the changepoints.

Regularizing changepoints

As stated earlier, Prophet will place 25 potential changepoints in the first 80% of the time series by default. To control Prophet's automatic changepoint detection, you can modify both of these values with the `n_changepoints` and `changepoint_range` arguments during model instantiation. For example, changing the number of potential changepoints to five is done like this:

```
model = Prophet(seasonality_mode='multiplicative',
                yearly_seasonality=4,
                n_changepoints=5)
```

This results in five evenly spaced potential changepoints in the first 80% of the data, as shown here:

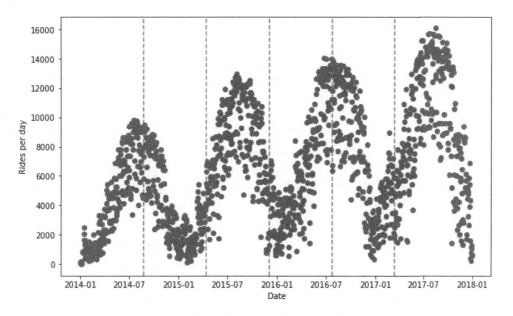

Figure 7.5 – Five potential changepoints

Or, you could instead force all 25 changepoints to lie not in the first 80% of data, but rather in the first 50%:

```
model = Prophet(seasonality_mode='multiplicative',
                yearly_seasonality=4,
                changepoint_range=.5)
```

Now, we see the potential changepoints are placed only in the first half of the data range:

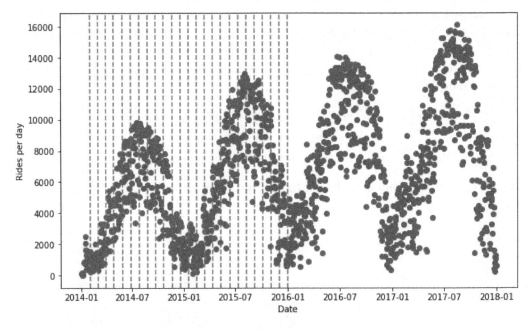

Figure 7.6 – Changepoints in the first 50% of data

You can, of course, use both of these arguments in one model. And in both cases, it is important to remember that you're not instructing Prophet to place changepoints at these locations, only *potential* changepoints. It will still try to force as many of them as possible to zero, and indeed both cases do leave us with predicted trends that are nearly identical to the example we built with default values.

Also, remember that Prophet will never place a changepoint in the future. This is why by default Prophet will only use the first 80% of data—to prevent it from choosing a poor changepoint with few upcoming data points with which to correct its mistake. Prophet will, however, estimate future changepoints when creating uncertainty intervals; so, a model that features many large changepoints will also see greater forecast uncertainty.

In general, setting changepoints at very late moments in the series has a higher likelihood of overfitting. To see why, I have built a two-year forecast of the Divvy data and forced Prophet to choose just one changepoint, placed in the final two months of data. During November, the number of rides per day drops quickly as usage declines in winter. Prophet saw this decline and decided it must be a negative trend change and so adjusted its future predictions accordingly:

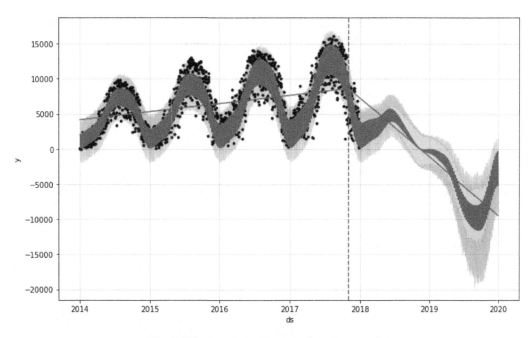

Figure 7.7 – Prophet with a very late changepoint

I may be no better at predicting the future than Prophet is, but I've got a high degree of confidence that Prophet's forecast in this case is not going to be very accurate in the future.

With all that said, you should not need to adjust the number of changepoints or the changepoint range very often. The defaults almost always work out very well. If you find Prophet is either overfitting or underfitting the changepoints, it is better to control this through regularization. Just as we did in *Chapter 4, Seasonality*, and *Chapter 5, Holidays*, we use the **prior scale** for regularization.

If you recall from *Chapter 4, Seasonality*, and *Chapter 5, Holidays*, the prior scale is used to control the flexibility of Prophet. A model that is too flexible has a high chance of overfitting the data, that is, modeling too much noise in addition to the true signal. A model that is not flexible enough has a high chance of underfitting the data or of not capturing all of the available signal.

By default, both `seasonality_prior_scale` and `holidays_prior_scale` were set to `10`. `changepoint_prior_scale`, however, is by default set to `0.05`. But just as with the seasonality and holidays prior scales, increasing this value will make the trend more flexible, and decreasing it will make the trend less flexible. Reasonable values are typically in the range of `0.001` to `0.5`.

Let's fit and plot a model with `changepoint_prior_scale` increased to 1. This should allow Prophet's trend to have a great deal of flexibility:

```
model = Prophet(seasonality_mode='multiplicative',
                yearly_seasonality=4,
                changepoint_prior_scale=1)
model.fit(df)
forecast = model.predict()
fig = model.plot(forecast)
add_changepoints_to_plot(fig.gca(), model, forecast)
plt.show()
```

Here, we can see that Prophet's trend is now wildly overfitting:

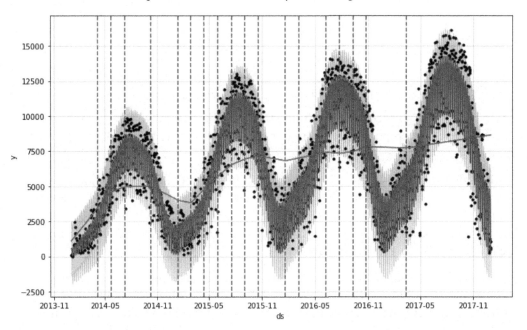

Figure 7.8 – Prophet with too little trend regularization

When we loosen the regularization parameter, Prophet starts overfitting the trend line and tries to capture some of the yearly seasonality. We have given Prophet too much flexibility with its trend fit.

On the other hand, let's now see what happens when we regularize too strictly. In this example, we decrease `changepoint_prior_scale` from the default down to `0.007`:

```
model = Prophet(seasonality_mode='multiplicative',
                yearly_seasonality=4,
                changepoint_prior_scale=.007)
model.fit(df)
forecast = model.predict()
fig = model.plot(forecast)
add_changepoints_to_plot(fig.gca(), model, forecast)
plt.show()
```

With the reduced `changepoint_prior_scale`, the following plot shows Prophet's trend to not be flexible enough:

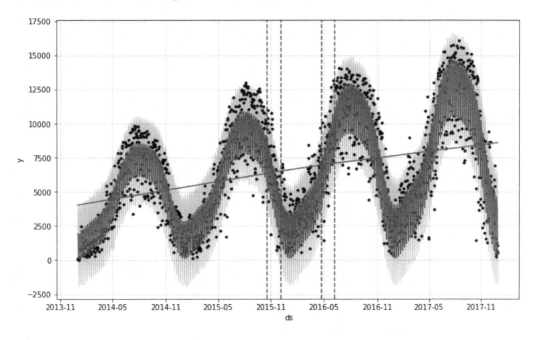

Figure 7.9 – Prophet with too much trend regularization

Compare *Figure 7.9* with *Figure 7.2* at the beginning of this chapter. Although the locations of the changepoints in *Figure 7.9* are roughly the same as in *Figure 7.2*, the magnitudes of the changepoints have been constrained too much with the regularization levels we used. That bend that was evident in *Figure 7.2* is now so minor in *Figure 7.9* that it is hard to spot.

There is one more way to control the changepoints in Prophet: by specifying your own custom changepoint locations. We're going to look at a new data set to explore this topic, the Instagram account of soccer player James Rodríguez, `@jamesrodriguez10`. This data was collected on November 22, 2019.

Specifying custom changepoint locations

James Rodríguez is a Colombian soccer player who played in both the 2014 and 2018 World Cups. He was a standout player in both Cups but won the Golden Boot award in 2014 for scoring more goals than any other player in the competition. I chose his account because it exhibits some very interesting behavior that would be extremely difficult to model without changepoints:

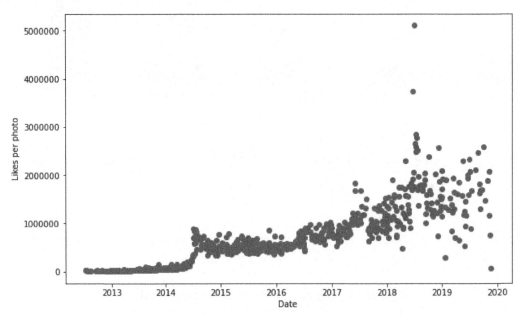

Figure 7.10 – James Rodríguez's Instagram likes per day

The number of likes his Instagram posts get is gradually increasing over time. But there are two notable spikes, in the summers of 2014 and 2018 when he was playing in the World Cup. It is clear that the spike in 2014 resulted in a significant trend change. The number of likes his posts were getting increased dramatically during the World Cup and dropped afterwards, but not to the same baseline as before. He had gained a large number of new followers during this period and consistently earned more likes per post as a result.

Similarly, in 2018, his profile saw a large summer spike in likes during the World Cup, but it is not clear that there was a significant trend change after the tournament ended. Also, you can see another spike in the summer of 2017. On July 11 of that year, Rodríguez announced that he had signed up with a new team, Bayern Munich. We'll include this fact in our model as well.

To model this behavior, we need to first account for the special events of the World Cups and the new team announcement. We will do this by creating custom holidays for them. And second, we need to account for the trend changes; we'll accomplish this by setting custom trend changepoints. There does not appear to be much seasonality in the data so to simplify our model, we'll just instruct Prophet not to fit any.

We already have our necessary imports completed, so we first need to load the data into our Prophet DataFrame:

```
df = pd.read_csv('instagram_jamesrodriguez10.csv')
df['Date'] = pd.to_datetime(df['Date'])
df.columns = ['ds', 'y']
```

Next, we need to create a DataFrame for the special events. This is the same procedure you learned in *Chapter 5*, *Holidays*. We have three events to add in this case, the 2014 World Cup, the 2017 signing for Bayern Munich, and the 2018 World Cup. Each event must have a name in the 'holiday' column and the date in the 'ds' column.

The two World Cups took place over 31 days each, so we'll specify the first date and an 'upper_window' of 31. We'll leave the 'lower_window' at 0. For the last event, signing with a new team, we'll give it a two-week window to be generous that the effect of signing for Bayern Munich impacted his posts for the next several days:

```
wc_2014 = pd.DataFrame({'holiday': 'World Cup 2014',
                        'ds':pd.to_datetime(['2014-06-12']),
                        'lower_window': 0,
                        'upper_window': 31})
wc_2018 = pd.DataFrame({'holiday': 'World Cup 2018',
                        'ds':pd.to_datetime(['2018-06-14']),
```

```
                        'lower_window': 0,
                        'upper_window': 31})
signing = pd.DataFrame({'holiday': 'Bayern Munich',
                        'ds':pd.to_datetime(['2017-07-11']),
                        'lower_window': 0,
                        'upper_window': 14})
special_events = pd.concat([wc_2014, wc_2018, signing])
```

Now, we need to specify our custom changepoints. We can simply pass Prophet a list of dates. Any date that pandas will recognize as a valid datetime format can be used:

```
changepoints = ['2014-06-12',
                '2014-07-13',
                '2017-07-11',
                '2017-07-31',
                '2018-06-14',
                '2018-07-15']
```

For each of those special events, we are adding one potential changepoint at the beginning of the event and one at the end. The rationale behind this decision is that we need to account for the fact that likes per photo will follow a certain trend, proportional to the number of followers of the account, until the trend is upset by a special event.

During the special event, the number of followers will increase at a much higher rate, and so the number of likes per photo will also increase, requiring a new trendline. After the event concludes, the dramatic rate of new followers will slow, so we need a third trendline at this point—resulting in three different trend slopes with two trend changepoints connecting them.

With our special events created and our potential changepoints determined, we next instantiate our Prophet object while passing it these special events and changepoints. For this example, we'll set the seasonality to multiplicative. This is count data and as discussed in *Chapter 4, Seasonality*, count data is often multiplicative.

However, there is an argument for using additive in this case—it is possible that the increased likes came from non-followers who visited Rodríguez's profile due to the World Cup but did not subsequently follow, which would be an additive effect, as opposed to increased activity from current followers, possibly due to Instagram's algorithmic feed ordering, which would be a multiplicative effect. In either case, the following procedure is the same.

We decided to simplify our model by removing seasonalities, so we'll set both `yearly_seasonality` and `weekly_seasonality` to `False`. You may be wondering why we bothered to set `seasonality_mode` if we don't have any seasonalities—this is because `seasonality_mode` affects the holidays as well.

Finally, we set the prior scale for the changepoints to `1` because we want to loosen the regularization a bit (feel free to experiment on your own with this number; I found the default to be too restrictive on this data), and pass our list of changepoints to the `changepoints` argument:

```
model = Prophet(seasonality_mode='multiplicative',
                holidays=special_events,
                yearly_seasonality=False,
                weekly_seasonality=False,
                changepoint_prior_scale=1,
                changepoints=changepoints)
```

We now continue as in the previous examples by calling the `fit` and `predict` methods on our model. We are not predicting into the future in this example, but if you wanted to you would need to add any future special events that you expect. Lastly, let's plot both our forecast and our components to observe the results:

```
model.fit(df)
forecast = model.predict()
fig = model.plot(forecast)
add_changepoints_to_plot(fig.gca(), model, forecast)
plt.show()
fig2 = model.plot_components(forecast)
plt.show()
```

First up is our forecast:

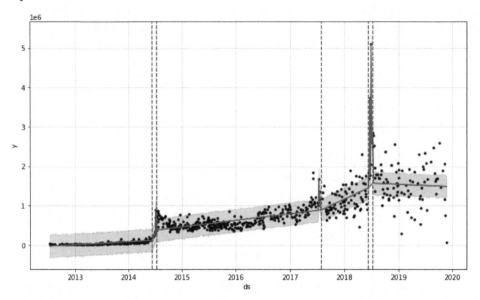

Figure 7.11 – James Rodríguez forecast

Despite the simplifications we made in our model, the trend is a remarkably good fit. Now let's look at our components plot:

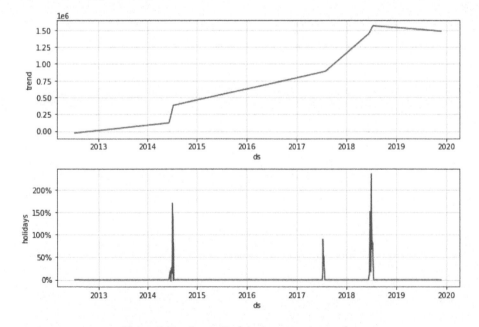

Figure 7.12 – James Rodríguez components plot

You can see from the holidays plot that both World Cups provided a roughly 200% increase in likes per post on James Rodríguez's account. When he signed for Bayern Munich, he saw a more modest, though still impressive, doubling of likes. And the trend line reflects these changes.

During each World Cup, he saw a rapid rise in the number of likes per post before the rate of increase of likes slowed while maintaining a higher baseline than before the event. Prophet determined that two changepoints for before and after each World Cup were necessary but found that the new team announcement only had one significant change in the trend.

There is one more way to handle changepoint locations, a hybrid technique blending custom changepoints with Prophet's default behavior. In this method, you would create an evenly spaced grid of changepoints, as Prophet does by default, and enrich it with your custom changepoints. Let's do one more example to see how to do this.

In Prophet's source code, there is a class method for creating the grid of potential changepoints called `set_changepoints`. This method is called automatically during the `fit` command if no changepoints have already been specified. The following function mimics that `set_changepoints` method to allow us to create a grid of potential changepoints outside the Prophet class. We will also need to import the numpy library for use in this function:

```python
import numpy as np


def set_changepoints(df, n_changepoints=25,
                     changepoint_range=.8):
    df = df.sort_values('ds').reset_index(drop=True)
    hist_size = int(np.floor(df.shape[0] * \
                             changepoint_range))
    if n_changepoints + 1 > hist_size:
        n_changepoints = hist_size - 1
        print('n_changepoints greater than number of '+
              'observations. Using {}.'\
              .format(n_changepoints))
    if n_changepoints > 0:
        cp_indexes = (np.linspace(0,
                                  hist_size - 1,
                                  n_changepoints + 1).
                      round().astype(np.int))
```

```
        changepoints = df.iloc[cp_indexes]['ds'].tail(-1)
    else:
        # set empty changepoints
        changepoints = pd.Series(pd.to_datetime([]),
                                 name='ds')
    return changepoints
```

This function requires three arguments. The first is your Prophet DataFrame with the `'ds'` and `'y'` columns. The second argument is the number of changepoints to create, defaulting to the same value of 25 as Prophet uses, and the third argument is the changepoint range, again defaulting to Prophet's value of .8. This returns a pandas series of potential changepoint locations. You simply then append your custom changepoints to it.

Using this function, let's create five evenly-spaced changepoints in the first 80% of the data, and then enrich the automatic changepoints with our six special event changepoints from the previous example:

```
changepoints = set_changepoints(df, 5, .8)
new_changepoints = pd.Series(pd.to_datetime(['2014-05-02',
                                             '2014-08-25',
                                             '2017-07-31',
                                             '2018-06-14',
                                             '2018-06-04',
                                             '2018-07-03']))
changepoints = changepoints.append(new_changepoints)
changepoints = \
changepoints.sort_values().reset_index(drop=True)
```

Now, let's recreate our previous model, but this time send it our new list of changepoints:

```
model = Prophet(seasonality_mode='multiplicative',
                holidays=special_events,
                yearly_seasonality=False,
                weekly_seasonality=False,
                changepoint_prior_scale=1,
                changepoints=changepoints)
model.fit(df)
forecast = model.predict()
```

```
fig = model.plot(forecast)
add_changepoints_to_plot(fig.gca(), model, forecast)
plt.show()
```

And now we can see that Prophet has used many more changepoints than before:

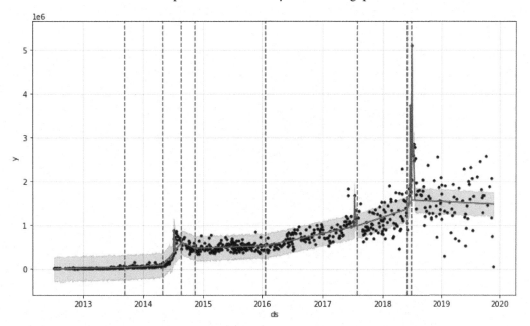

Figure 7.13 – Forecast with hybrid automatic/manual potential changepoints

We also have a trend line that is very flexible; perhaps it is overfitting? That is a decision for you, the analyst, to determine. But as a demonstration of how to blend your own custom changepoints with an automatically selected grid of potential changepoints, this example will suffice.

Summary

In this chapter, you learned how to control the fit of the trend line by using changepoints. First, you used Divvy data to see how Prophet automatically selects potential changepoint locations and how you can control this by modifying the default number of potential changepoints and the changepoint range.

Then you learned a more robust way to control Prophet's changepoint selection through regularization. Just as with seasonality and holidays, changepoints are regularized by setting the prior scale. You then looked at the Instagram data of James Rodríguez and learned how to model the increase in likes per post he received both during and after the World Cups of 2014 and 2018. Finally, you learned how to blend these two techniques and enrich an automatically selected grid of potential changepoints with your custom changepoint locations.

In the next chapter, we will again look at the Divvy data, but this time we'll include the additional columns for temperature and weather conditions in order to learn how to include additional regressors in a Prophet forecast.

8
Additional Regressors

In your first model in *Chapter 2, Getting Started with Facebook Prophet*, you forecasted carbon dioxide levels at Mauna Loa, using only the date, but no other information, to predict future values. Later, in *Chapter 5, Holidays*, you learned how to add holidays as additional information to further refine your predictions of bicycle ridership in the Divvy bike share network in Chicago.

The way holidays are implemented in Prophet is actually a special case of adding a binary regressor. In fact, Prophet includes a generalized method for adding any additional regressor, both binary and continuous.

In this chapter, you'll enrich your Divvy dataset with weather information by including it as an additional regressor. First, you will add binary weather conditions to describe the presence or absence of sun, clouds, or rain, and then next you will bring in continuous temperature measurements. Using additional regressors can allow you to include more information to inform your models, which leads to greater predictive power. In this chapter, you will learn about the following topics:

- Adding binary regressors
- Adding continuous regressors
- Interpreting the regressor coefficients

Technical requirements

The data files and code for examples in this chapter can be found at
`https://github.com/PacktPublishing/Forecasting-Time-Series-Data-with-Facebook-Prophet`.

Adding binary regressors

The first thing to consider with **additional regressors**, whether binary or continuous, is that you must have known future values for your entire forecast period. This isn't a problem with holidays because we know exactly when each future holiday will occur. All future values must either be known, as with holidays, or must have been forecast themselves separately. You must be careful though when building a forecast using data that itself has been forecast: the error in the first forecast will compound the error in the second forecast, and the errors will continuously pile up.

If one variable is much easier to forecast than another, however, then this may be a case where these stacked forecasts do make sense. A **hierarchical time series** is an example case where this may be useful: you may find good results by forecasting the more reliable daily values of one time series, for instance, and using those values to forecast hourly values of another time series that is more difficult to predict.

In the examples in this chapter, we are going to use a weather forecast to enrich our Divvy forecast. This additional regressor is possible because we generally do have decent weather forecasts available looking ahead a week or so. In other examples in this book, in which we have used Divvy data, we often forecasted out a full year. In this chapter though, we will only forecast out 2 weeks. Let's be generous to Chicago's weather forecasters and assume that they'll provide accurate forecasts in this time frame.

To begin, let's import our necessary packages and load the data:

```
import pandas as pd
import matplotlib.pyplot as plt
from fbprophet import Prophet

df = pd.read_csv('divvy_daily.csv')
```

Please refer to *Figure 4.6* in *Chapter 4, Seasonality*, for a plot of the rides per day in this data. *Figure 4.7* in *Chapter 4, Seasonality*, showed an excerpt of the data contained in this file. So far in this book, we always excluded the two columns for weather and temperature in this dataset, but we'll use them this time around. For our first example, let's consider the weather conditions. By counting the number of times each condition occurred in the dataset, we can see their frequencies:

```
print(df.groupby('weather')['weather'].count())
```

The output of the preceding `print` statement is as follows:

```
weather
clear            41
cloudy           1346
not clear        2
rain or snow     69
Name: weather, dtype: int64
```

Figure 8.1 – Count of weather conditions in the Divvy dataset

By grouping the data by weather and aggregating by count, we can see the number of days each condition was reported. `clear` weather occurred on `41` days, and `cloudy` weather was by far the most common, with `1346` occurrences. `not clear` was only reported twice, and `rain or snow` `69` times.

Now that we understand what data we're working with, let's load it into our DataFrame. We'll also load the temperature column even though we won't use it until the next example when we look at **continuous** columns, those in which the value may exist along a continuum.

To load the weather column, we will use pandas' `get_dummies` method to convert it into four **binary** columns for each unique weather condition, meaning that each column will be a `1` or a `0`, essentially a flag indicating whether the condition is present:

```
df['date'] = pd.to_datetime(df['date'])
df.columns = ['ds', 'y', 'temp', 'weather']
df = pd.get_dummies(df, columns=['weather'], prefix='',
                    prefix_sep='')
```

We can display the first five rows of our DataFrame at this point to see what the preceding code has done:

```
df.head()
```

The output of the `head` statement should appear as follows:

	ds	y	temp	clear	cloudy	not clear	rain or snow
0	2014-01-01	95	19.483158	0	0	0	1
1	2014-01-02	111	16.833333	0	0	0	1
2	2014-01-03	6	-5.633333	1	0	0	0
3	2014-01-04	181	30.007735	0	0	0	1
4	2014-01-05	32	16.756250	0	0	0	1

Figure 8.2 – DataFrame with dummy weather columns

You can now see that each unique value in the `weather` column has been converted to a new column. Let's instantiate our model now, setting the seasonality mode to multiplicative and the yearly seasonality to have a Fourier order of 4, as we did in previous chapters.

We will also add in our additional regressors using the `add_regressor` method. As arguments to this method, you must pass the name of the regressor, which is the name of the corresponding column in your DataFrame. You may also use the `prior_scale` argument to regularize the regressor, just as you did with holidays, seasonalities, and trend changepoints. If no prior scale is specified, then `holidays_prior_scale` will be used, which defaults to `10`.

You may also specify whether the regressor should be additive or multiplicative. If nothing is specified, then the regressor adopts that stated in `seasonality_mode`. Lastly, the method has a `standardize` argument, which, by default, takes the string `'auto'`. This means that the column will be standardized if not binary. You can instead explicitly set standardization by setting it to either `True` or `False`. In this example, all defaults will work out great.

To make it clear, I'll explicitly state all arguments in only the first `add_regressor` call and, for the remaining, we will only state the name of the regressor and otherwise accept all default values.

We must make one `add_regressor` call for each additional regressor but note that we are leaving the regressor for `cloudy` out. For Prophet to get accurate forecast results, this isn't strictly necessary. However, because including all four binary columns will introduce **multicollinearity**, this makes interpreting the individual effect of each condition difficult, so we will exclude one of them. However, Prophet is fairly robust to multicollinearity in additional regressors, so it shouldn't affect your final results significantly.

When we called `pd.get_dummies` earlier, we could have specified the `drop_first=True` argument to exclude one of the conditions, but I decided not to so we could choose for ourselves which column to exclude. The cloudy condition is by far the most frequent, so by excluding it we are essentially stating that `cloudy` is the *default* weather condition and the other conditions will be stated as deviations from it:

```python
model = Prophet(seasonality_mode='multiplicative',
                yearly_seasonality=4)
model.add_regressor(name='clear',
                    prior_scale=10,
                    standardize='auto',
                    mode='multiplicative')
model.add_regressor('not clear')
model.add_regressor('rain or snow')
```

Now, remembering that we need future data for our additional regressors and we're only going to forecast out two weeks, we need to artificially reduce our training data by two weeks to simulate having two future weeks of weather data but no ridership data. To do that, we'll need to import `timedelta` from Python's built-in `datetime` package.

Using Boolean indexing in pandas, we will create a new DataFrame for training data, called `train`, by selecting all dates that are less than the final date (`df['ds'].max()`) minus two weeks (`timedelta(weeks=2)`):

```python
from datetime import timedelta


# Remove final 2 weeks of training data
train = df[df['ds'] < df['ds'].max() - timedelta(weeks=2)]
```

At this point, we are essentially saying that our data ends not on December 31, 2017 (as our `df` DataFrame does), but on December 16, 2017, and that we have a weather forecast for those two missing weeks. We now fit our model on this `train` data and create our `future` DataFrame with 14 days.

At this point, we need to add those additional regressor columns into our `future` DataFrame. Because we created that `train` DataFrame instead of modifying our original `df` DataFrame, those *future* values for the weather are stored in `df` and we can take them to use in our `future` DataFrame. Finally, we will predict on the future.

The forecast plot is going to look similar to our previous Divvy forecasts, so let's just skip it and go straight to the components plot:

```
model.fit(train)

future = model.make_future_dataframe(periods=14)
future['clear'] = df['clear']
future['not clear'] = df['not clear']
future['rain or snow'] = df['rain or snow']
forecast = model.predict(future)

fig2 = model.plot_components(forecast)
plt.show()
```

This time, you will see a new subplot included with the other components. The following image is a crop of the full components plot and only shows the yearly seasonality and this new component:

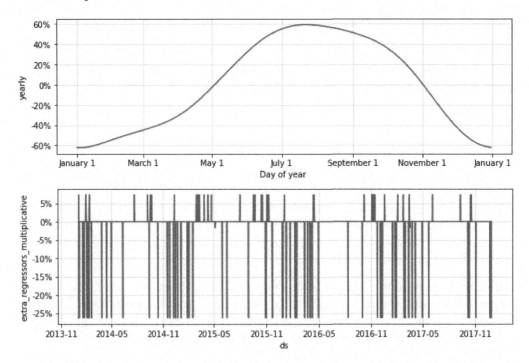

Figure 8.3 – Cropped components plot of binary additional regressors

The trend, weekly seasonality, and yearly seasonality, which were cropped out, look much the same as we've seen before with this dataset. However, we have a new addition to the components plot, called `extra_regressors_multiplicative`. Had we specified some of those regressors as additive, we would see a second subplot here, called `extra_regressors_additive`.

On dates where the value is at 0%, these are our *baseline* dates when the weather was cloudy, which we left out of the additional regressors. The other dates are those where the weather deviated from cloudy, which we included. We'll take a more in-depth look at this in a bit. But first, let's bring temperature into our model and add a **continuous regressor**.

Adding continuous regressors

In this example, we will take everything from the previous example and simply add in one more regressor for temperature. Let's begin by looking at the temperature data:

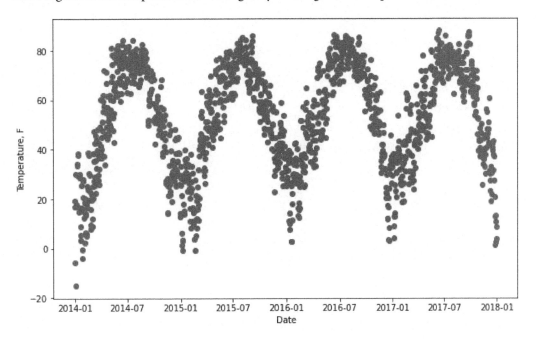

Figure 8.4 – Chicago temperature over time

There's nothing too surprising about the preceding plot; daily temperatures rise in summer and fall in winter. It does look a lot like *Figure 4.6* from *Chapter 4, Seasonality*, but without that increasing trend. Clearly, Divvy ridership and the temperature rise and fall together.

Adding temperature, a continuous variable, is no different than adding binary variables. We simply add another add_regressor call to our Prophet instance, specifying 'temp' for the name, and also including the temperature forecast in our future DataFrame. As we did before, we are fitting our model on the train DataFrame we created, which excludes the final 2 weeks' worth of data. Finally, we plot the components to see what we've got:

```
model = Prophet(seasonality_mode='multiplicative',
                yearly_seasonality=4)
model.add_regressor('temp')
model.add_regressor('clear')
model.add_regressor('not clear')
model.add_regressor('rain or snow')

model.fit(train)

future = model.make_future_dataframe(periods=14)
future['temp'] = df['temp']
future['clear'] = df['clear']
future['not clear'] = df['not clear']
future['rain or snow'] = df['rain or snow']
forecast = model.predict(future)

fig2 = model.plot_components(forecast)
plt.show()
```

Now, the extra_regressors_multiplicative plot shows the same fluctuations that our temperature plot displayed:

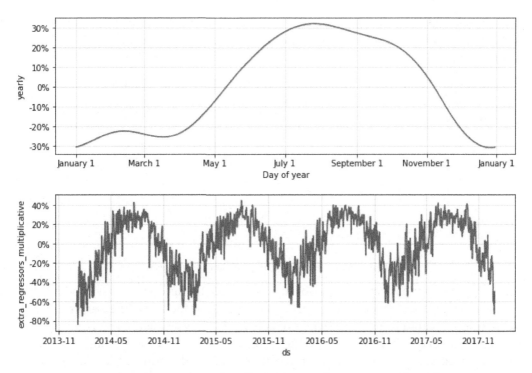

Figure 8.5 – Cropped components plot of both binary and continuous additional regressors

Also note that in *Figure 8.2*, the `yearly` plot peaked at 60% effect magnitude. However, now we can see that temperature accounts for some of that effect. The `yearly` plot in *Figure 8.4* shows a peak 30% effect, while the `extra_regressors_multiplicative` plot shows a 40% increase on certain summertime dates and a massive 80% decrease in ridership on certain wintertime dates. To break this down further, we now need to discuss how to interpret this data.

Interpreting the regressor coefficients

Now let's look at how to inspect the effects of these additional regressors. Prophet includes a package called `utilities`, which has a function that will come in handy here, called `regressor_coefficients`. Let's import it now:

```
from fbprophet.utilities import regressor_coefficients
```

Using it is straightforward. Just pass the model as an argument and it will output a DataFrame with some helpful information about the extra regressors included in the model:

```
regressor_coefficients(model)
```

Let's take a look at this DataFrame:

	regressor	regressor_mode	center	coef_lower	coef	coef_upper
0	temp	multiplicative	53.423706	0.012282	0.012282	0.012282
1	clear	multiplicative	0.000000	0.109030	0.109030	0.109030
2	not clear	multiplicative	0.000000	-0.032346	-0.032346	-0.032346
3	rain or snow	multiplicative	0.000000	-0.205786	-0.205786	-0.205786

Figure 8.6 – The regressor coefficients DataFrame

It features a row for each extra regressor in your model. In this case, we have one for temperature and three more for the weather conditions we included. The `regressor_mode` column naturally will have strings of either `additive` or `multiplicative`, depending upon the effect of each specific regressor on `'y'`. The mean value of the pre-standardized regressor (the raw input data) is saved in the `center` column. If the regressor wasn't standardized, then the value will be zero.

The `coef` column is the one you really want to pay attention to. It denotes the expected value of the coefficient. That is, the expected impact on `'y'` of a unit increase in the regressor. In the preceding DataFrame, the `coef` for `temp` is 0.012282. This coefficient tells us that for every degree higher than the `center` (53.4, in this case), the expected effect on ridership will be 0.012282, or a 1.2% increase.

For the `rain or snow` row, which is a binary regressor, it tells us that on those rainy or snowy days, then ridership will be down 20.6% compared to cloudy days, as that was the regressor we left out. Had we included all four weather conditions, to interpret this value, you would say ridership would be down 20.6% compared to the value predicted for the same day if modeled without including weather conditions.

Finally, the columns for `'coef_lower'` and `'coef_upper'` indicate the lower and upper bounds, respectively, of the uncertainty interval around the coefficient. They are only of interest if `mcmc_samples` is set to a value greater than zero. **Markov chain Monte Carlo** samples, or **MCMC** samples, is a topic you'll learn about in *Chapter 10, Uncertainty Intervals*. If `mcmc_samples` is left at the default value, as in these examples, `'coef_lower'` and `'coef_upper'` will be equal to `coef`.

Now, to conclude, we can plot each of these extra regressors individually with the `plot_forecast_component` function we first used in *Chapter 5, Holidays*. After importing it from Prophet's `plot` package, we will loop through each regressor in that `regressor_coefficients` DataFrame to plot it:

```
from fbprophet.plot import plot_forecast_component


fig, axes = plt.subplots(
                    len(regressor_coefficients(model)),
                    figsize=(10, 15))
for i, regressor in enumerate(
    regressor_coefficients(model)['regressor']):
    plot_forecast_component(model,
                        forecast,
                        regressor,
                        axes[i])
plt.show()
```

We plotted all of those as subplots in one figure, resulting in the following diagram:

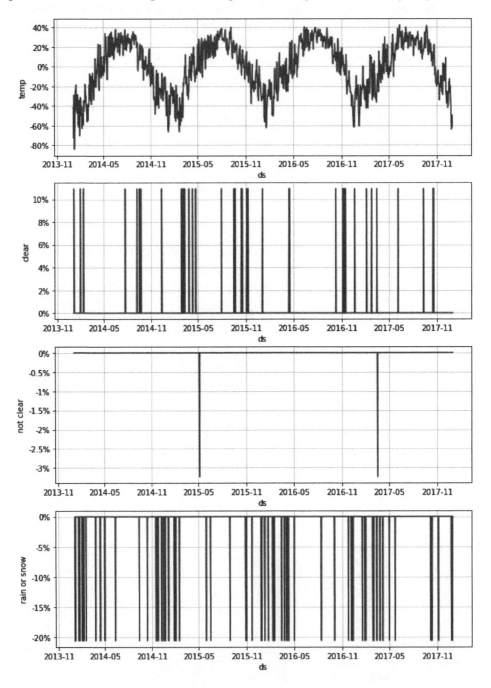

Figure 8.7 – Divvy extra regressor plots

At last, we can visualize the effects of these regressors individually. The magnitudes of these plots should match the `coef` values in the DataFrame created with the `regressor_coefficients` function seen in *Figure 8.5*.

One final note regarding additional regressors in Prophet: they are always modeled as a linear relationship. This means that, for example, our extra regressor of temperature, which was found to increase ridership by 1.2% for every degree increase, is modeling a trend that will continue to infinity. That is, if the temperature were to spike to 120 degrees Fahrenheit, there's no way for us to change the linear relationship and inform Prophet that ridership will probably decrease now that it's getting so hot outside.

Although this is a limitation of Prophet as currently designed, in practice it is not always a great problem. A linear relationship is very often a good proxy for the actual relationship, especially for a small range of data, and will still add a lot of additional information to your model to enrich your forecasts.

Summary

In this chapter, you learned a generalized method to add any additional regressors beyond the holidays, which you learned how to add earlier. You learned that adding both binary regressors, such as weather conditions, and continuous regressors, such as temperature, use the same `add_regressor` method. You also learned how to use the `regressor_coefficients` function in Prophet's `utilities` package to inspect the effects of your additional regressors.

Although you may now want to add all sorts of extra regressors to your forecasts, you also learned that Prophet requires all additional regressors to have defined values going into the future or else there's no information to inform a forecast. This is why we only forecasted 2 weeks out when using weather data.

In the next chapter, we are going to look at how Prophet handles outliers and how you can exert greater control over the process yourself.

9
Outliers and Special Events

An **outlier** is any data point that lies significantly away from the other data points along one or multiple different axes. Outliers may be incorrect data, such as resulting from a miscalibrated sensor producing invalid data, or even a finger slip on the keyboard during data entry, or they may be accurately recorded data that happens to wildly miss historical trends for various reasons, such as if a tornado passed over a wind speed sensor.

These uncharacteristic measurements will sway any statistical or machine learning model, and so correcting outliers is a challenge throughout data science and statistics. Fortunately, Prophet is generally robust to mild outliers. With extreme outliers though, there are two problems Prophet can experience: one problem with seasonality and another with uncertainty intervals.

In this chapter, you'll see examples of both of these problems and learn how to alleviate their effects on your forecast. You'll also learn a few techniques to automate outlier detection, and lastly, you'll apply a lesson learned in *Chapter 7, Trend Changepoints*, to keep the outliers in your model but instruct Prophet not to modify the trend or seasonalities to fit them.

This chapter will cover the following topics:

- Correcting outliers that cause seasonality swings
- Correcting outliers that cause wide uncertainty intervals
- Detecting outliers automatically
- Modeling outliers as special events

Technical requirements

The data files and code for the examples in this chapter can be found at
`https://github.com/PacktPublishing/Forecasting-Time-Series-Data-with-Facebook-Prophet`.

Correcting outliers that cause seasonality swings

We'll be using a new dataset in this chapter to look at outliers: the average number of likes per day of posts on National Geographic's Instagram account, `@NatGeo`. This data was collected on November 21, 2019.

I've chosen this dataset because it exhibits several significant outliers, which are marked in the following plot:

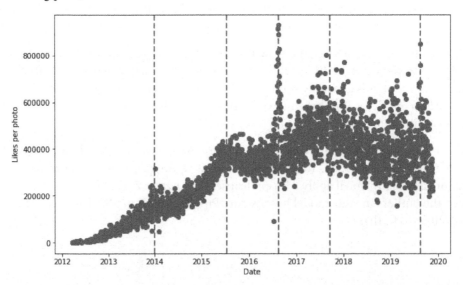

Figure 9.1 – Outliers on National Geographic's Instagram account

Each dashed vertical line indicates a moment where the time series deviated significantly. The second line from the left indicates a radical trend change in the summer of **2015** but the other four lines indicate outliers, with the last two outliers spanning across wide time ranges. We'll specifically be looking at the line occurring in mid-**2016**, in August to be precise. This represents the most extreme outliers. The **2014** set of outliers can be safely ignored, as they do not affect the forecast too much. The **2017** and **2019** outliers look like they may be seasonal effects, so we'll let the yearly seasonality capture them.

As it turns out, in September 2016, National Geographic published a book, *@NatGeo: The Most Popular Instagram Photos*. It seems that in the month prior to this, National Geographic undertook some marketing activities, which boosted the number of likes on its Instagram account.

As we saw in *Chapter 7, Trend Changepoints*, James Rodríguez's account also saw an increased number of likes during his World Cup appearances. However, in his case, these events were followed by higher baselines of likes at their conclusion—a significant trend change had occurred. In contrast, National Geographic's August marketing work did not produce a lasting trend change, although it did increase the number of likes.

The spike represents the first type of problem outliers can cause in Prophet: they can dominate a seasonality curve. Let me show you what I mean by plotting a Prophet forecast. Let's make our imports, load the data, and plot the forecast. We'll use multiplicative seasonality and dampen the Fourier order of the yearly seasonality down to 6:

```python
import pandas as pd
import matplotlib.pyplot as plt
from fbprophet import Prophet
from fbprophet.plot import add_changepoints_to_plot


df = pd.read_csv('instagram_natgeo.csv')
df['Date'] = pd.to_datetime(df['Date'])
df.columns = ['ds', 'y']


model = Prophet(seasonality_mode='multiplicative',
                yearly_seasonality=6)
model.fit(df)
future = model.make_future_dataframe(periods=365 * 2)
forecast = model.predict(future)
fig = model.plot(forecast)
plt.show()
```

These outliers have caused Prophet to model a spike in likes each August:

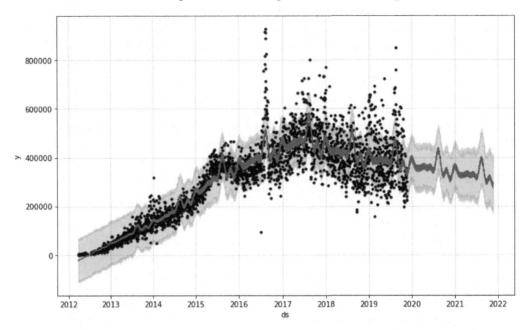

Figure 9.2 – NatGeo forecast with outliers

It's true that August in **2013**, **2015**, **2017**, and **2019** also saw periods of increased likes, but the even years did not. Some seasonality would be expected but not this much. To make matters worse, this effect reverberates forever into the future. You can see how significant an effect this is by looking at the yearly seasonality plot:

```
from fbprophet.plot import plot_yearly

plot_yearly(model, figsize=(10.5, 3.25))
plt.show()
```

Here, you can see the August peak clearly:

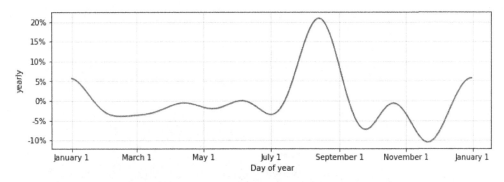

Figure 9.3 – Prophet yearly seasonality with outliers

While attempting to fit a yearly seasonality to those outliers in **2016**, Prophet has allowed August to contribute a boost of more than 20% to the number of expected likes. We see those frequent August boosts, so we do want Prophet to model them, but the **2016** anomaly is dominating.

The solution is simply to remove the points. Prophet handles missing data very well, so introducing a small gap won't pose any issues. In *Chapter 3, Non-Daily Data*, you learned how to handle regular gaps by removing those gaps from the future DataFrame as well. In this case though, as long as we have August data for other years, we don't need to take that precaution.

It seems that the first major outlier was on July 29 and the final one was on September 1, so we'll exclude data between those dates using pandas' Boolean indexing:

```
df2 = df[(df['ds'] < '2016-07-29') |
         (df['ds'] > '2016-09-01')]
```

This new df2 is identical to our original df, just excluding those outliers. Let's build the same Prophet model as before but just switch out the previous DataFrame, df, for this new one, df2:

```
model = Prophet(seasonality_mode='multiplicative',
                yearly_seasonality=6)
model.fit(df2)
future = model.make_future_dataframe(periods=365 * 2)
forecast = model.predict(future)
fig = model.plot(forecast)
plt.show()
```

You can see the month-long gap in August 2016 in this plot. The forecast simply passes through it:

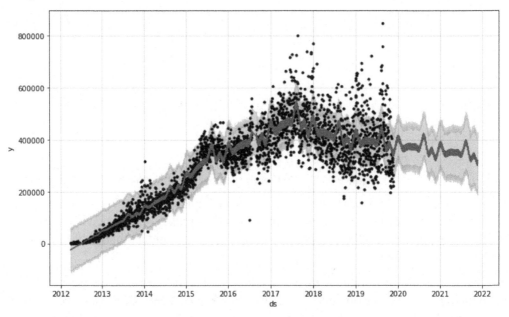

Figure 9.4 – NatGeo forecast with outliers removed

This new forecast also shows significant seasonality, but we do expect this as NatGeo's likes are frequently higher in the summer. To quantify the difference between this forecast and the previous, let's also plot the yearly seasonality:

```
plot_yearly(model, figsize=(10.5, 3.25))
plt.show()
```

It's a very similar shape to *Figure 9.3*, but with a less exaggerated August peak:

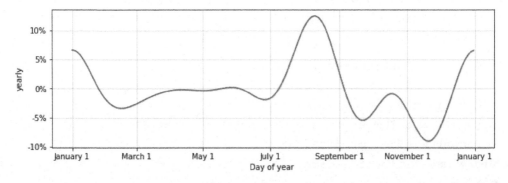

Figure 9.5 – Prophet yearly seasonality with outliers removed

Now, the August peak is almost halved; it is just over 10% of a boost. This is much closer to what would be expected without the external (and non-repeating) shock of the marketing push before the release of National Geographic's book.

Now, let's look at the second type of outlier issue.

Correcting outliers that cause wide uncertainty intervals

In the first type of outlier we looked at, the problem was that the seasonality was affected and forever changed `yhat` in the forecast (if you remember from *Chapter 2, Getting Started with Facebook Prophet*, `yhat` is the predicted value for future dates contained in Prophet's `forecast` DataFrame). In this second problem, `yhat` is minimally affected but the uncertainty intervals widen dramatically.

To simulate this issue, we need to modify our NatGeo data a bit. Let's say that Instagram introduced a bug in their code that capped likes to 100,000 per post. It somehow went unnoticed for a year before being fixed, but unfortunately, all likes above 100,000 were lost. Such an error would look like this:

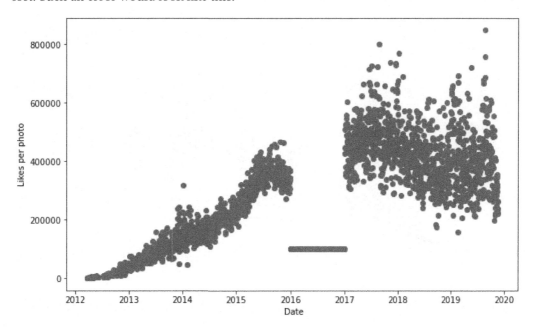

Figure 9.6 – Capped likes on National Geographic's Instagram account

You can simulate this new dataset yourself with the following code:

```
df3 = df.copy()
df3.loc[df3['ds'].dt.year == 2016, 'y'] = 100000
```

This sets all the likes on all posts in 2016 to 100,000. To see what problem this causes, let's again build the same model as before:

```
model = Prophet(seasonality_mode='multiplicative',
                yearly_seasonality=6)
model.fit(df3)
future = model.make_future_dataframe(periods=365 * 2)
forecast = model.predict(future)
fig = model.plot(forecast)
add_changepoints_to_plot(fig.gca(), model, forecast)
plt.show()
```

We're adding the changepoints to the plot in this example because that is exactly where the error is introduced, as seen in the following graph:

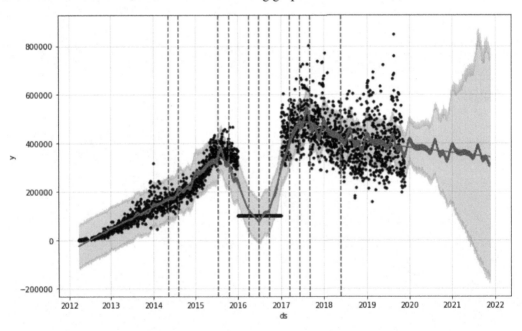

Figure 9.7 – NatGeo forecast with outliers

The future uncertainty explodes going forward. In the previous example, Prophet modeled the outliers with seasonality, adding the extreme data to the yearly seasonality component. In this example though, Prophet is modeling the outliers with trend changepoints. The seasonality is unaffected.

We'll fully discuss uncertainty in *Chapter 10, Uncertainty Intervals*, but briefly, what Prophet does is look at the frequency and magnitude of historical changepoints, and model future uncertainty assuming that future changepoints may occur with the same frequency and magnitude. So, dramatic historical changepoints, as you can see in *Figure 9.7*, will cause dramatic future uncertainty as Prophet is unsure whether they will occur again.

The solution, fortunately, is the same as in the previous situation: simply remove the bad data. In the previous example, we removed the rows from our DataFrame that contained bad data; but in this example, we'll set the `'y'` value to None:

```
df3.loc[df3['ds'].dt.year == 2016, 'y'] = None
```

This makes no difference to our trend or seasonalities. Where it does make a difference is that now, instead of skipping over those dates in the `forecast` DataFrame, it predicts the values on those dates. You can see this in the forecast plot coming up in *Figure 9.8*. Instead of a straight prediction line passing through the missing data, it follows the seasonality.

Let's rebuild our model again, using this `df3` DataFrame:

```
model = Prophet(seasonality_mode='multiplicative',
                yearly_seasonality=6)
model.fit(df3)
future = model.make_future_dataframe(periods=365 * 2)
forecast = model.predict(future)
fig = model.plot(forecast)
add_changepoints_to_plot(fig.gca(), model, forecast)
plt.show()
```

Compared to *Figure 9.7*, we have now tamed that forecast uncertainty, as seen in the following plot:

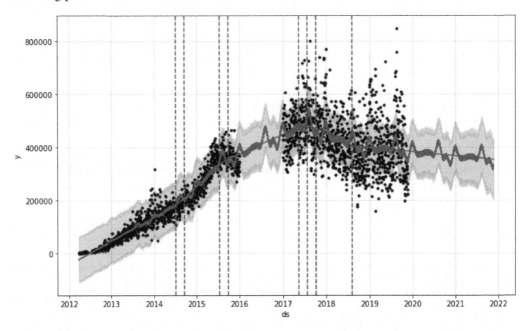

Figure 9.8 – NatGeo forecast with outliers removed

As mentioned before, we have missing data in 2016 but Prophet still made a prediction and plotted the predicted values. This is the result of setting those missing values to None instead of deleting them. Compare *Figure 9.8* with *Figure 9.4*, where the missing data has no predicted values and the plot passes right through them in a straight line.

Mathematically, it makes no difference to your future forecast, it just applies predicted values to those that were missing. It is entirely up to your preference whether you want these missing values to be predicted in the future DataFrame or ignored.

Detecting outliers automatically

In these examples so far, we detected outliers with a simple visual inspection of the data and applied common sense. In a fully automated setting, defining logical rules for what we as humans do intuitively can be difficult. Outlier detection is a good use of an analyst's time as we humans are able to use much more intuition, domain knowledge, and experience than a computer can. But as Prophet was developed to reduce the workload of analysts and automate as much as possible, we'll examine a couple of techniques to identify outliers automatically.

Winsorizing

The first technique is called **Winsorization**, named after the statistician Charles P. Winsor. It is also sometimes called **clipping**. Winsorization is a blunt tool and tends not to work well with non-flat trends. Winsorization requires the analyst to specify a percentile; all data above or below that percentile is forced to the value at the percentile.

Trimming is a similar technique, except that the extreme values are removed. The difference between these techniques can be seen in this simple example, in which the outliers are the two most extreme points on each side of the three plots:

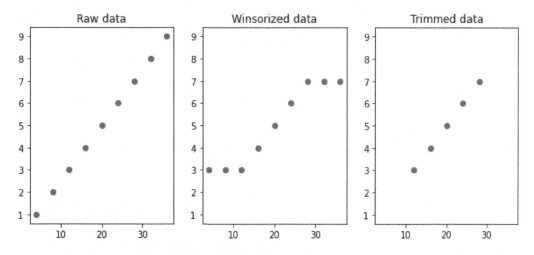

Figure 9.9 – Winsorization versus trimming

> **Tip**
>
> In statistics, the word *stationary* means that the mean, variance, and autocorrelation structure do not change over time. In time series with a *flat trend*, the mean does not change over time and so one (and possibly each) requirement of stationarity is met. With stationary data, outliers may often be replaced by the mean value, but this technique typically does not work, with time series lacking a flat trend due to the stationarity requirement.
>
> To take a concrete example, refer back to *Figure 2.2*, from *Chapter 2, Getting Started with Facebook Prophet*, looking at the Keeling Curve of carbon dioxide levels at Mauna Loa, and imagine replacing one of the final values, say in 2015, with the mean of the full dataset. This would result in an absurdly low value of about 360 in 2015, a value not seen in 20 years.

Let's look at how to apply Winsorization to our National Geographic data. The **SciPy** `stats` package has a Winsorization tool, so we'll use that. Note that we are dropping all null values, as those are not handled with this function. We are setting the lower limit to `0`, so no values are affected at the lower bound, and the upper limit to `.05`, so the upper fifth percentile is affected:

```
from scipy import stats


df4 = df.copy().dropna()
df4['y'] = stats.mstats.winsorize(df4['y'],
                                  limits=(0, .05), axis=0)
```

The Winsorized National Geographic data appears thus, with affected data points marked with an **x**:

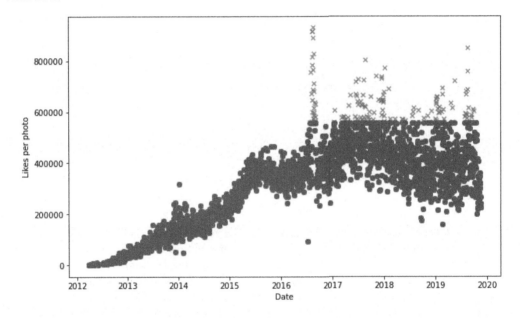

Figure 9.10 – Winsorized data

Standard deviation

Since Winsorization limits are set with percentiles, there is no account taken of natural variance in the data. That is, some datasets are very tight around a mean value and some are very spread out. Setting a percentile limit would not take this into account. So, instead of using percentiles, sometimes using standard deviation makes more sense. This is very similar to Winsorization and can have identical effects if the limits are set carefully.

When we Winsorized in the previous section, we forced the outliers to take on the value at the upper limit. In this case, we will simply remove the outliers. We are using the `zscore` function in the SciPy `stats` package to eliminate those data points lying `1.65` standard deviations above the mean; in a normal distribution, this upper value would demarcate 95% of the data, the same limit we set previously:

```
df5 = df.copy().dropna()
df5 = df5[(stats.zscore(df5['y']) < 1.65)]
```

In this case, the two techniques have nearly identical results, except that here we are trimming the data:

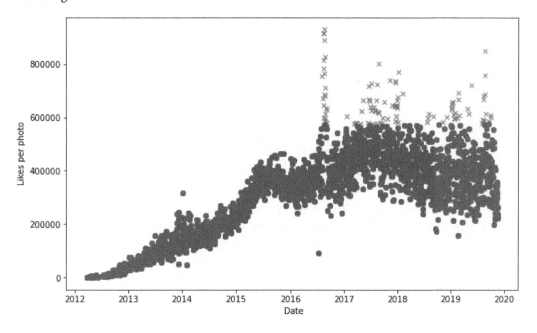

Figure 9.11 – Data trimmed with standard deviation

This method is also a poor fit when the data features a trend. Obviously, points lying later in a time series with an upward trend are more likely to be trimmed than those lying earlier. The next technique takes this into account.

Moving average

We just looked at the number of standard deviations away from the mean of the entire dataset and saw why it fails when there is a trend. In this method, we will use a moving average so that we're essentially localizing our mean and standard deviation calculations and only applying them to data points that are temporally near each other.

In this example, we will trim both the upper and lower bounds of the data, again using the `1.65` value for standard deviation as before. The analyst also needs to decide upon a window size. This is the number of surrounding data points to collect together for calculation. Set it too small and a group of outliers together will not be removed. Set it too large and we approach the previous technique of ignoring the trend.

Let's use `300` here. We use pandas `rolling` method to find the mean and standard deviation using a rolling window. Then, we calculate the upper and lower bounds using these values and filter our DataFrame with those bounds:

```
df6 = df.copy().dropna()


df6['moving_average'] = df6.rolling(window=300,
                                    min_periods=1,
                                    center=True,
                                    on='ds')['y'].mean()
df6['std_dev'] = df6.rolling(window=300,
                             min_periods=1,
                             center=True,
                             on='ds')['y'].std()
df6['lower'] = df6['moving_average'] - 1.65 * \
                df6['std_dev']
df6['upper'] = df6['moving_average'] + 1.65 * \
                df6['std_dev']


df6 = df6[(df6['y'] < df6['upper']) & \
          (df6['y'] > df6['lower'])]
```

We are now getting more refined outlier removal, as can be seen in the following graph:

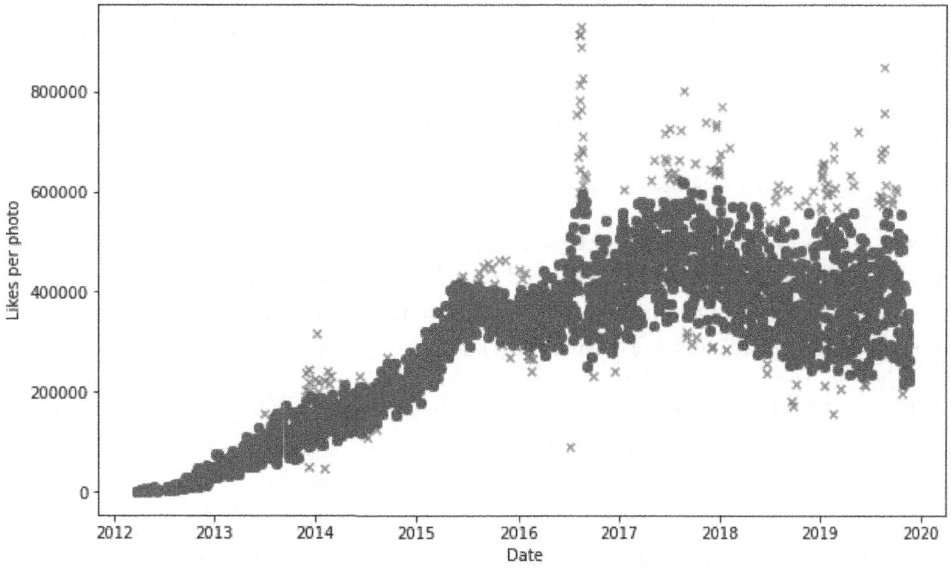

Figure 9.12 – Data trimmed with the moving average

The strong advantage of this method is that it takes into account the trend.

Error standard deviation

The final method we will consider is the most precise of all. Let's go back to the question of defining an outlier: it is a value that you don't expect. Intuitively, we knew this when we visually inspected the data and removed points. So, how do you tell the computer what to expect? You build a forecast, of course.

Prophet's `forecast` DataFrame makes predictions in the `yhat` column, but it also includes columns for `yhat_upper` and `yhat_lower`. These uncertainty intervals are by default set to 80%, but you'll learn in *Chapter 10, Uncertainty Intervals*, how to modify them. If we accept any errors contained within the uncertainty intervals, we can declare an outlier to be anything that falls outside of these bounds, as it would be unexpected.

In fact, the moving average is a crude forecasting technique; the previous method was indeed removing outliers based upon deviation in the error term. By using Prophet to identify the error, we allow seasonality and other effects to be included in our expected results.

As the most precise method available, this is unfortunately also the most prone to overfit. If you do wish to use this approach, be sure to tread carefully on new datasets and make sure you like the results before fully automating it. That said, let's see how to code it.

Our approach will be to first remove null values to avoid downstream issues when comparing our `forecast` DataFrame to our raw DataFrame:

```
df7 = df.copy().dropna().reset_index()
```

Next, we build a Prophet model on this data, including strong regularization to be sure we don't overfit. Note that there is no need to predict on the future. We include the `interval_width` argument here to increase the uncertainty interval to better align with our previous examples; we'll cover this parameter in the next chapter:

```
model = Prophet(seasonality_mode='multiplicative',
                yearly_seasonality=6,
                seasonality_prior_scale=.01,
                changepoint_prior_scale=.01,
                interval_width=.90)
model.fit(df7)
forecast = model.predict()
```

Finally, we create a DataFrame that excludes those values where the y value was either greater than `yhat_upper` or lower than `yhat_lower`. These would be our outliers:

```
df8 = df7[(df7['y'] > forecast['yhat_lower']) &
          (df7['y'] < forecast['yhat_upper'])]
```

The final DataFrame would then be used to build a whole new Prophet model, without needing to worry about outliers. This is what our data looks like now:

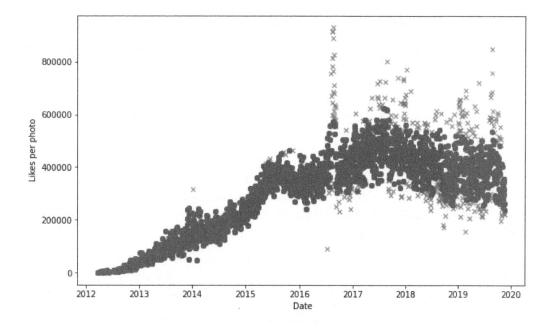

Figure 9.13 – Data trimmed with error from the forecast

We have certainly removed what would plausibly be considered outliers. Had we used Prophet's default uncertainty interval, then outlier removal may have been a bit too aggressive in this case. If you compare *Figure 9.13* with the data plots of our other methods, this one appears to be the most surgical, for instance, by allowing high values that we would expect in the summer but removing those that are uncharacteristically high.

Using this method makes the implicit assumption that the data is stationary and has a constant variance, which appears to be a poor assumption throughout the full National Geographic dataset but a fair assumption when considering only the data after 2016. The full data becomes more spread out as time advances. This is why more data points were dropped at later dates than earlier dates—just one more thing to consider when using this method.

Throughout this chapter, we have been removing outliers from our data. However, there is one technique you can use to keep those outliers around if you believe they provide some valuable signal in your model but you want to control the effect. This technique uses the holiday functionality in Prophet. Let's see how to do it next.

Modeling outliers as special events

There is one final way to work with outliers in Prophet; it's a technique we used with James Rodríguez's data in *Chapter 7, Trend Changepoints*—we can declare the outliers as a special event, essentially a holiday. By putting the outliers into the holidays DataFrame, we essentially instruct Prophet to apply trend and seasonality as if the data points were not outliers and capture the additional variation beyond trend and seasonality in the holiday term.

This could be useful if you know the extreme observations are due to some external factor that you do not expect to repeat. Such external factors could be the World Cup or a large marketing campaign but may also be mysterious and unknown. You could keep the data in your model but essentially disregard it. An added benefit is that you can simulate what would happen if the event repeats.

We'll again use the National Geographic data, but this time label that August 2016 series of outliers as a holiday. If those additional likes were due to a marketing campaign surrounding the release of their book, we can predict what would happen if they repeated a similar marketing campaign at a later date.

We covered the creation of custom holidays in *Chapter 5, Holidays*, so this first step should be a review. We are simply creating two holidays for our August 2016 marketing event and an identical hypothetical June 2020 marketing event.

Note that both events have the same name, `'Promo event'`, so Prophet knows to apply the same effect to each. They're both the same number of days long, although they needn't be—the holiday effects for each day of the hypothetical event will match the effects for each day of the measured event.

If the hypothetical event is shorter, the effects will simply cease early. If the hypothetical event is longer though, the effects will cease once the length of the measured event is reached.

We begin by defining the promotions the same way we define holidays:

```
promo = pd.DataFrame({'holiday': 'Promo event',
                      'ds': pd.to_datetime(['2016-07-29']),
                      'lower_window': 0,
                      'upper_window': 34})
future_promo = pd.DataFrame({'holiday': 'Promo event',
                             'ds': pd.to_datetime(['2020-06-01']),
                             'lower_window': 0,
```

```
                                'upper_window': 34})

promos = pd.concat([promo, future_promo])
```

Next, we build our model using the same parameters as throughout this chapter, except sending the first `promo` DataFrame to the `holidays` argument:

```
model = Prophet(seasonality_mode='multiplicative',
                holidays=promo,
                yearly_seasonality=6)
model.fit(df)
future = model.make_future_dataframe(periods=365 * 2)
forecast = model.predict(future)
fig = model.plot(forecast)
plt.show()
```

Our forecast perfectly models that spike of outliers, without either letting seasonality get out of control (the first problem we looked at in this chapter), or letting the future uncertainty explode (the second problem):

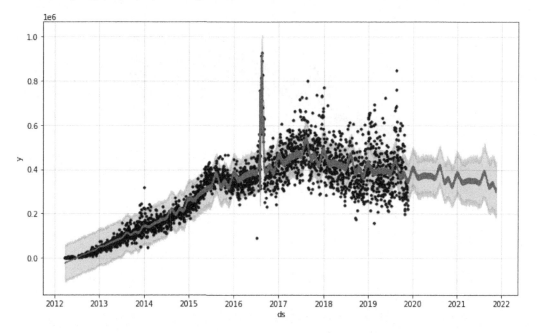

Figure 9.14 – NatGeo forecast with outliers modeled as special events

To conclude this example, let's try one more model but this time include that hypothetical promotional event:

```
model = Prophet(seasonality_mode='multiplicative',
                holidays=promos,
                yearly_seasonality=6)
model.fit(df)
future = model.make_future_dataframe(periods=365 * 2)
forecast = model.predict(future)
fig = model.plot(forecast)
plt.show()
```

This is the future forecast National Geographic could expect if they had duplicated the promotional activities in 2020:

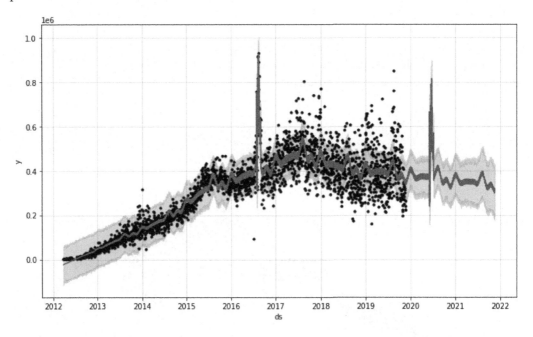

Figure 9.15 – NatGeo forecast with a hypothetical promotional event

With just one instance of the holiday to train with, Prophet has perfectly matched the holiday effects to the data, which is a good recipe for overfitting. If National Geographic had several similar marketing events, they could model all of them as the same holiday, which would average out the effects.

Summary

Outliers are a fact of any data analysis, but they do not always have to cause headaches. Prophet is very robust at handling most outliers without any special consideration, but sometimes problems can arise. In this chapter, you learned about the two problems most common with outliers in Prophet: uncontrolled seasonality and exploding uncertainty intervals.

In both cases, simply removing the data is the best approach to solving the problem. As long as data exists in other periods of the seasonality cycles for those gaps where data was removed, Prophet has no problem finding a good fit.

You also learned several automated outlier detection techniques, from the basic techniques of Winsorization and trimming, which tend not to work well on time series exhibiting a trend, to the more advanced technique of stacking forecasts and using errors in the first model to remove outliers for the second model.

Finally, you learned how to model outliers as special events, which has much the same effect as removing the data while retaining the information from that outlier. This technique has the advantage of allowing you to simulate a similar shock to your time series occurring in the future.

In the next chapter, we'll look at a related concept to outliers: uncertainty intervals.

10
Uncertainty Intervals

Forecasting is essentially predicting the future, and with any prediction, there will necessarily be a particular amount of uncertainty. Quantifying this uncertainty provides the analyst with an understanding of how reliable their forecasts are and it provides the manager with the confidence to stake a lot of capital on a decision.

Prophet was designed from the ground up with uncertainty modeling in mind. Although you interact with it in either **Python** or **R**, the underlying model is built in the **Stan** programming language, a probabilistic language that allows Prophet to perform **Bayesian sampling** in an efficient manner to provide a deeper understanding of the uncertainty in the model, and thus the business risk of the forecast.

There are three sources of uncertainty that contribute to the total uncertainty in your Prophet model:

- Uncertainty in the trend
- Uncertainty in the seasonality, holidays, and additional regressors
- Uncertainty due to noise in the data

The last of these is an inherent attribute of whatever data you are using, but the first two can be modeled and examined. In this chapter, you will learn how Prophet models uncertainty, how you can control it in your model, and how you can use these uncertainty estimations to quantify risk. Specifically, this chapter will cover the following topics:

- Modeling uncertainty in trends
- Modeling uncertainty in seasonality

Technical requirements

The data files and code for examples in this chapter can be found at `https://github.com/PacktPublishing/Forecasting-Time-Series-Data-with-Facebook-Prophet`.

Modeling uncertainty in trends

You may have noticed in different component plots throughout this book that the trend shows uncertainty bounds, while the seasonality curves do not. By default, Prophet only estimates uncertainty in the trend, plus uncertainty due to random noise in the data. The noise is modeled as a normal distribution around the trend and trend uncertainty is modeled with **maximum a posteriori (MAP) estimation**.

MAP estimation is an optimization problem that is solved with **Monte Carlo simulations**. Named after the famous casino in Monaco, the Monte Carlo method uses repeated random sampling to estimate an unknown value, usually used when closed-form equations are either non-existent or computationally difficult.

In *Chapter 5*, *Holidays*, we talked about **prior distributions**, or the **probability distribution** of an estimate prior to receiving additional information about it. In MAP estimation, you are estimating the central tendency of a **posterior distribution**, or a probability distribution after learning additional information. In the case of trend uncertainty, the posterior distribution is the distribution of estimated trend values at each date, after seeing the training data. This optimization problem is a relatively quick problem to solve. So, even with many iterations, it can complete in just seconds during the `model.fit(df)` call.

Let's take a look at some Prophet parameters you can use to control trend uncertainty. We're going to use a new dataset in this chapter, the number of crimes reported to the Baltimore police department each day from 2011 through 2019. Let's begin with our imports and loading the data:

```
import pandas as pd
import matplotlib.pyplot as plt
from fbprophet import Prophet
from fbprophet.plot import add_changepoints_to_plot
import numpy as np
np.random.seed(42)


df = pd.read_csv('baltimore_crime.csv')
df.columns = ['ds', 'y']
```

If you plot the data, you'll see that it has a relatively flat trend, seasonality, and a couple of outliers. In particular, I have drawn a dashed line in the following graph at the level of 250 crimes per day and there are two data points above this line:

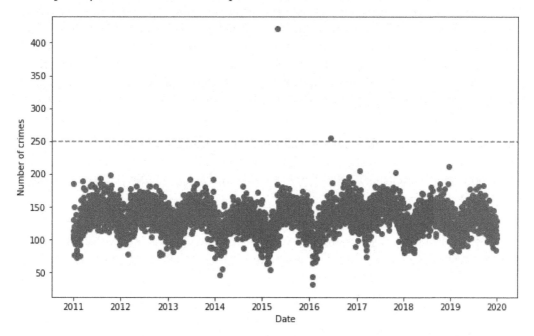

Figure 10.1 – Baltimore crime data

Although those points probably won't affect our forecasts as much as the outliers did in the National Geographic data we looked at in *Chapter 9, Outliers and Special Events*, let's remove them and avoid any potential issues as follows:

```
df.loc[df['y'] > 250, 'y'] = None
```

> **Important note**
>
> Notice that we imported NumPy and set the random seed. MAP estimation is a deterministic calculation in Prophet, so you will always get the same trend repeatedly (or, very nearly the same trend, due to slight differences in how different machines handle floating-point numbers). However, the uncertainty intervals are randomly created. With 1,000 iterations, they should be very similar in repeated experiments, but if no random seed was set, then your plots may not match those in this book. Furthermore, **MCMC (Markov chain Monte Carlo)** sampling, which is used when uncertainty estimates for seasonality are needed and will be discussed later in this chapter, does add randomness to the trend calculations. Setting the random seed will ensure that you get the same results as this book.

The biggest source of uncertainty in the Prophet forecast comes from the potential for future trend changes. When training the model, Prophet runs through many Monte Carlo simulations for the future, assuming that future trend changepoints will occur with the same frequency and magnitude of historical changepoints. For this reason, a time series with large magnitude changepoints in its history will see very wide trend uncertainty; we saw this with the National Geographic Instagram data in *Figure 9.7* from *Chapter 9, Outliers and Special Events*.

The number of Monte Carlo simulations Prophet runs through is set with the `uncertainty_samples` argument during model instantiation. By default, it is set to `1000`, so Prophet simulates 1,000 different future trend lines and uses these to estimate uncertainty.

Let's build our first model explicitly stating this default by setting `uncertainty_samples=1000` when instantiating our model. We'll then fit, create a five-year forecast, and plot it with the changepoints. For this Baltimore crime data, we can keep all the other defaults during model instantiation:

```
model = Prophet(uncertainty_samples=1000)
model.fit(df)
future = model.make_future_dataframe(periods=365 * 5)
forecast = model.predict(future)
fig = model.plot(forecast)
```

```
add_changepoints_to_plot(fig.gca(), model, forecast)
plt.show()
```

It looks like crime in Baltimore was up in 2011 at the beginning of the dataset, dropped a bit over the next few years, and then rose again, before dropping. Prophet continues this trend onward into the future:

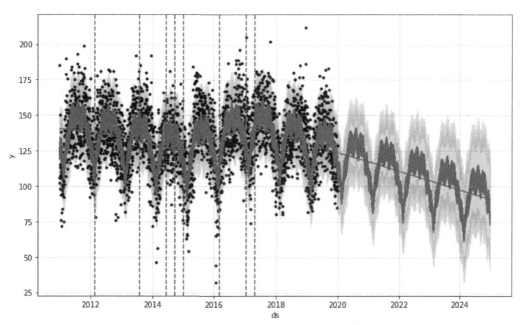

Figure 10.2 – Baltimore crime forecast with 1,000 uncertainty samples

The uncertainty (the lighter shaded area in the plot) exists throughout both the history and the future. Now, let's plot the components:

```
fig2 = model.plot_components(forecast)
plt.show()
```

The trend uncertainty only exists in the forecasted future; there is no uncertainty evident in the historical data:

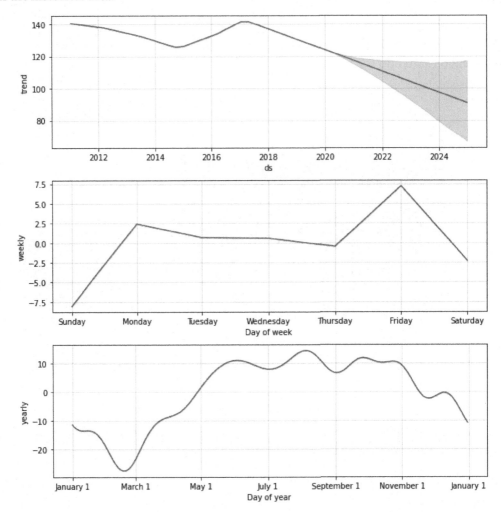

Figure 10.3 – Baltimore crime components plot with 1,000 uncertainty samples

This is because all historical uncertainty is attributed to noise. As I said earlier, the noise is modeled as a normal distribution around the prediction. As trend uncertainty is due to uncertainty with future trend changepoints, trend uncertainty only exists in the future. The total uncertainty seen in *Figure 10.2* is the noise uncertainty plus the trend uncertainty. Also, the Prophet team notes that their assumption that future trend changes will never be of greater magnitude than previous trend changes is a very limiting assumption, and so you should not expect to get extremely accurate coverage on uncertainty intervals.

When Prophet ran through those 1,000 iterations to estimate future trend changes, it saved each result in the `predictive_samples` attribute of the model. This is a dictionary with keys of `'yhat'` and `'trend'`, storing, respectively, the estimated values for the total prediction and the prediction of just the trend, for each iteration:

```
samples = model.predictive_samples(future)
```

By plotting `samples['trend']` against `future['ds']`, for each sample, you can see each of Prophet's 1,000 potential trend simulations:

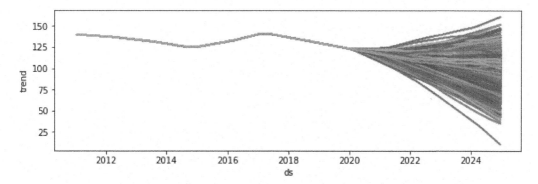

Figure 10.4 – Baltimore crime trend with 1,000 uncertainty samples

By default, Prophet has an uncertainty interval of 80%. Each of those 1,000 possible trend lines are equally probable within an 80% confidence level. Because future uncertainty is estimated from future potential changepoints, which are, in turn, estimated from previous changepoints, increasing or decreasing the number of previous changepoints through the use of `changepoint_prior_scale` will have a matching effect on uncertainty bounds.

It is usually unnecessary to change the number of uncertainty samples to anything other than the default. Increasing it will give you a better estimate of uncertainty, at the cost of computing time, but 1,000 samples is usually plenty to get a good estimate. Setting the argument to either `uncertainty_samples=0` or `uncertainty_samples=False` is a special case, though, which disables uncertainty estimation and speeds up calculations significantly.

The uncertainty level can be controlled through the `interval_width` argument. If you want more confidence in your uncertainty levels, you may want to increase this value; decreasing it will give you tighter limits but less confidence. Let's increase the width to `0.99`, for a 99% confidence level:

```
model = Prophet(interval_width=0.99)
model.fit(df)
future = model.make_future_dataframe(periods=365 * 5)
forecast = model.predict(future)
```

I'll only plot the trend, as that is where the effect of this change is most evident:

```
from fbprophet.plot import plot_forecast_component

plot_forecast_component(model,
                        forecast,
                        'trend',
                        figsize=(10.5, 3.25))
plt.show()
```

Compare the following diagram with the trend component in *Figure 10.3*:

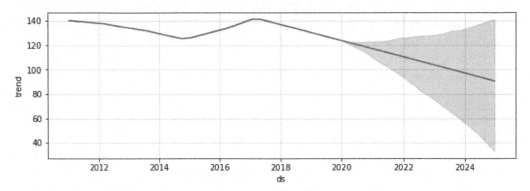

Figure 10.5 – Baltimore crime trend with a 99% uncertainty interval width

The width of uncertainty is much greater in this plot. Because we want higher confidence that the bounds contain the true trend, we have to expand the bounds to provide this higher certainty.

You've been modeling trend uncertainty throughout this book. But now you want to see uncertainty bounds in seasonality as well. In the next section, you'll learn how to accomplish this.

Modeling uncertainty in seasonality

MAP estimation is very fast, which is why it is Prophet's default mode, but it will not work with seasonalities, so a different method is needed. To model seasonality uncertainty, Prophet needs to use an MCMC method. A **Markov chain** is a model that describes a sequence of events, with the probability of each event depending upon the state in the previous event. Prophet models seasonal uncertainty with this chained sequence and uses the Monte Carlo method, which was described at the beginning of the previous section, to repeat the sequence many times.

The downside is that MCMC sampling is slow; on a macOS or Linux machine, you should expect fitting times of several minutes instead of several seconds. On a Windows machine, unfortunately, the PyStan API, which interfaces with Prophet's model in the Stan language, has upstream issues, meaning MCMC sampling is extremely slow. Depending upon the number of data points, fitting a model on a Windows machine can sometimes take several hours.

The Prophet team recommends that users on Windows machines work with Prophet in R or use Python in a Linux virtual machine. Another alternative is to use Google's Colab notebooks, which are similar to cloud-hosted Jupyter Notebooks. They are free to use and are built in Linux, so they do not face the PyStan issues that Windows does. You can access them at `https://colab.research.google.com/`.

With that caveat out of the way, let's see how to model uncertainty in seasonality. We will leave the default `1000` uncertainty samples that we've used so far and add a different argument for `mcmc_samples`. If you set this argument to `0`, Prophet will revert to MAP estimation and only provide uncertainty in the trend component, reverting to the models we created in the previous examples in this chapter. We will use 300 MCMC samples:

```python
model = Prophet(mcmc_samples=300)
model.fit(df)
future = model.make_future_dataframe(periods=365 * 5)
forecast = model.predict(future)
fig = model.plot(forecast)
add_changepoints_to_plot(fig.gca(), model, forecast)
plt.show()
```

After fitting and predicting, we plot the forecast. The first thing that may jump out at you is the number of changepoints, as can be seen in the following graph:

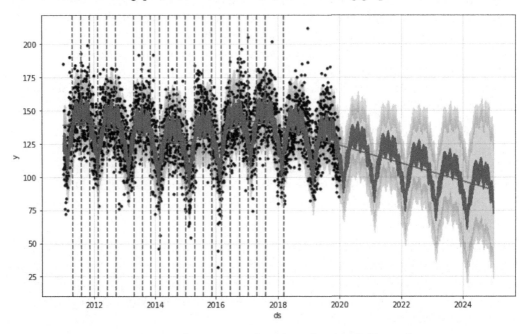

Figure 10.6 – Baltimore crime forecast with 300 MCMC samples

We'll deal with that changepoint issue in a bit. Now though, let's look at the components plot:

```
fig2 = model.plot_components(forecast)
plt.show()
```

You should now see uncertainty intervals around both the `weekly` and `yearly` seasonalities as follows:

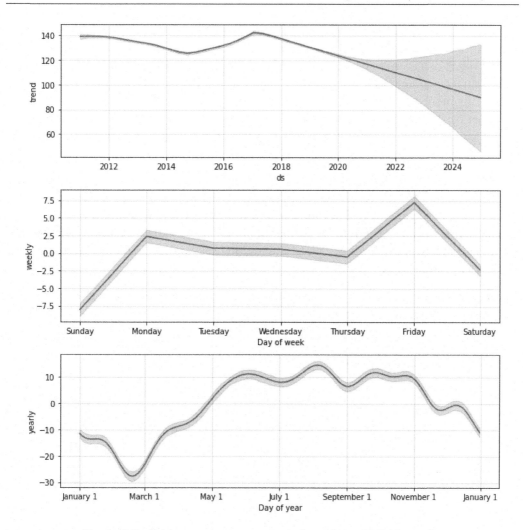

Figure 10.7 – Baltimore crime components plot with 300 MCMC samples

Had we added holidays or any additional regressors, you'd see uncertainty intervals there, too. Go ahead and try it out yourself, using the Divvy example from *Chapter 8, Additional Regressors*.

In this model, we accepted the default `uncertainty_samples=1000` argument and set `mcmc_samples=300`. When Prophet runs its MCMC method, it uses a total of four chains (although this value can be changed using the keyword `chains` argument in the `fit` call). The `mcmc_samples` argument is the total number of samples generated per chain. This is different to the `uncertainty_samples` argument, which is the total number of sampled trend lines to generate.

When `mcmc_samples=0`, Prophet will generate exactly the number of potential trend lines as defined in the `uncertainty_samples` argument. However, when `mcmc_samples` is any value greater than zero, Prophet will generate *at least* the number of potential trend lines as defined in the `uncertainty_samples` argument, but potentially more as it needs to have the same number of iterations per chain. That all may be rather confusing, but it is just a small technicality. The only practical effect you may notice is that `model.predictive_samples(future)` may have fractionally more rows than you specified in `uncertainty_samples`.

Now, let's get back to those changepoints. Why were there so many when performing MCMC sampling? If you remember from *Chapter 7, Trend Changepoints*, Prophet sets a high number of potential changepoints and tries to set their magnitude as low as possible. This works fine with MAP estimation. In a Bayesian analysis, however, as MCMC sampling is, there is a well-known phenomenon that causes the parameters not to shrink in the same way.

This is a plot of the changepoint magnitudes of our first model shown in *Figure 10.2*, and our most recent model, in *Figure 10.6*:

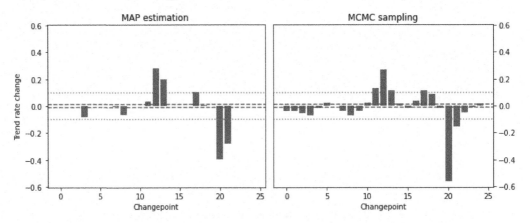

Figure 10.8 – Changepoint magnitudes resulting from different uncertainty estimations

The problem we have is not one of our modeling, just one of visualization. The two dashed lines in the preceding graphs show the default `0.01` threshold for plotting changepoint magnitudes in the `add_changepoints_to_plot` function (the dotted lines show an increased threshold of `0.1`).

Changepoints that extend beyond this line were plotted in *Figure 10.2*. The model plotted in *Figure 10.6* has many more changepoints extending beyond this line, so they are plotted, too. However, the extra changepoints cancel each other out. They are negative and then positive. The overall effect is that the trends in both *Figure 10.2* and *Figure 10.6* are nearly identical:

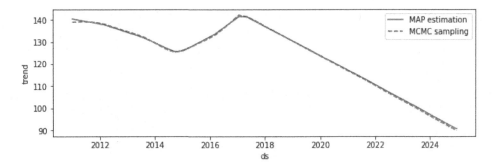

Figure 10.9 – Trend lines resulting from different changepoint uncertainty estimations

The lesson from this is not to worry too much about it. If you want a more reasonable number of changepoints on your plot, feel free to change the `threshold` argument when adding the changepoints. Here, we change it to `0.1`, the level marked in *Figure 10.8* with the dotted line:

```
fig = model.plot(forecast)
add_changepoints_to_plot(fig.gca(), model, forecast,
                         threshold=0.1)
plt.show()
```

Now we see a similar number of changepoints as follows:

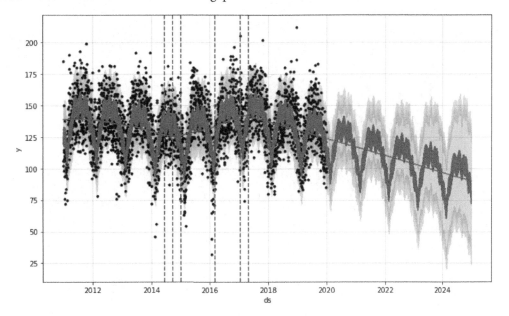

Figure 10.10 – Baltimore crime forecast with an increased changepoint threshold

They are different changepoints but remember that this is just an issue that cropped up with visualization. The final trend in both models was very similar. The slight differences that arise are due to the different statistical sampling techniques; neither technique is more correct than the other, they are both estimations of the data.

This isn't always the case though. Sometimes you'll see too many dramatic trend changes with MCMC sampling. If this happens, you can simply decrease your `changepoint_prior_scale` value and rein in those changepoint magnitudes a bit. For example, let's decrease it from the `0.05` default value we've been using down to `0.03`:

```
model = Prophet(changepoint_prior_scale=0.03,
                mcmc_samples=300)
model.fit(df)
future = model.make_future_dataframe(periods=365 * 5)
forecast = model.predict(future)
fig = model.plot(forecast)
add_changepoints_to_plot(fig.gca(), model, forecast,
                         threshold=0.1)
plt.show()
```

At this level, we have fewer significant changepoints than in *Figure 10.6*, as can be seen in the following graph:

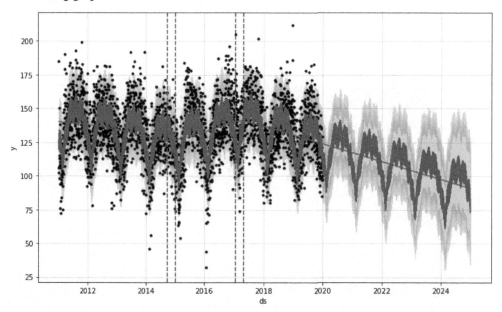

Figure 10.11 – Baltimore crime forecast with increased changepoint regularization

If we compare the trend lines, we see that this regularized line matches the original MAP estimation ever so slightly better:

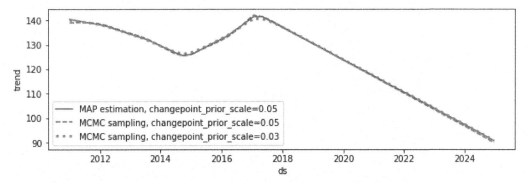

Figure 10.12 – Trend lines resulting from different changepoint prior scales

If you use MCMC sampling, just be sure to pay attention to the increased number of changepoints. If your trend line appears to be overfitting, you can simply reduce the changepoint prior scale to control it.

Summary

Uncertainty intervals are a vital tool for understanding your forecast. No prediction of the future can have absolute confidence. By explicitly stating the confidence level in your model, you provide your audience with an understanding of the risk involved in the model's predictions, to better guide their decisions.

In this chapter, you learned that all models built in previous chapters used MAP estimations to create confidence levels. This method requires less time to compute than the alternative, MCMC sampling, but can only model uncertainty in the trend component. Often, this is enough. However, for those times when you also need uncertainty stated for seasonality, holidays, or extra regressors, you also learned how to apply MCMC sampling in Prophet to build a more comprehensive model of uncertainty.

Finally, you learned of an inherent weakness of MCMC sampling in terms of its ability to apply regularization to trend changepoints. You will usually see a larger quantity of significant changepoints in a Prophet model built with MCMC sampling than one built with MAP estimation. It is for this reason that you learned to pay close attention to trend overfit when using MCMC sampling and to tune your changepoint prior scale accordingly.

In the next chapter, you'll learn about cross-validation in Prophet. You may be familiar with k-fold cross-validation from other machine learning applications; k-fold fails with time series. We will cover a different method, called forward chaining.

Section 3: Diagnostics and Evaluation

This final section will be about model evaluation and next steps. You will learn how to use Prophet's built-in performance metrics to compare different models in a statistically robust way and how to visualize their performance. Finally, the section will close out with some additional features of Prophet that could be used when deploying Prophet in real-world use cases, where updating models and sharing results are likely to be frequent occurrences.

This section comprises the following chapters:

- *Chapter 11, Cross-Validation*
- *Chapter 12, Performance Metrics*
- *Chapter 13, Productionalizing Prophet*

11
Cross-Validation

The concept of keeping training data and testing data separate is sacrosanct in machine learning and statistics. You should never train a model and test its performance on the same data. Setting data aside for testing purposes has a downside, though: that data has valuable information that you would want to include in training. **Cross-validation** is a technique that's used to circumvent this problem.

You may be familiar with **k-fold cross-validation**, but if you are not, we will briefly cover it in this chapter. K-fold, however, will not work on time series. It requires that the data be independent, an assumption that time series data does not hold. An understanding of k-fold will help you learn how forward-chaining cross-validation works and why it is necessary for time series data.

After learning how to perform cross-validation in Prophet, you will learn how to speed up the computing of cross-validation through Prophet's ability to parallelize several processes. All in all, this chapter will cover the following topics:

- Performing k-fold cross-validation
- Performing forward-chaining cross-validation
- Creating the Prophet cross-validation DataFrame
- Parallelizing cross-validation

Technical requirements

The data files and code for examples in this chapter can be found at
`https://github.com/PacktPublishing/Forecasting-Time-Series-Data-with-Facebook-Prophet`.

Performing k-fold cross-validation

We'll be using a new dataset in this chapter, the sales of an online retailer in the United Kingdom. This data has been anonymized, but it represents 3 years of daily sales amounts, as displayed in the following graph:

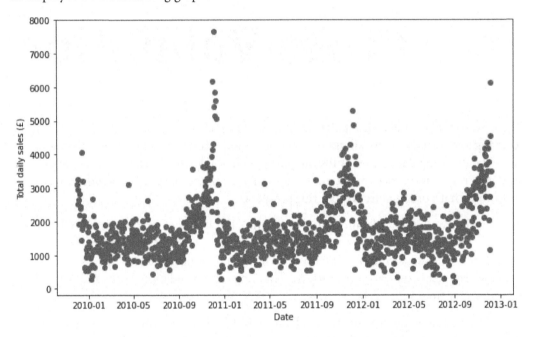

Figure 11.1 – Daily sales of an anonymous online retailer

This retailer has not seen dramatic growth over the 3 years of data, but it has seen a massive boost in sales at the end of the year. The main customer of this retailer is wholesalers, who typically make their purchases during the work week. This is why when we plot the components of Prophet's forecast, you'll see that Saturday and Sunday's sales are the lowest. We'll use this data to perform cross-validation in Prophet.

Before we get to modeling, though, let's first review traditional validation techniques to tune a model's hyperparameters and report performance. The most basic method is to take your full dataset and split it into three subsets: a **training set**, **validation set**, and **test set**, after randomly shuffling it around. This is sometimes called **hold-out** validation. Usually, the training set is the largest and the validation and testing sets are smaller. For example, a 60% / 20% / 20% split would look like this:

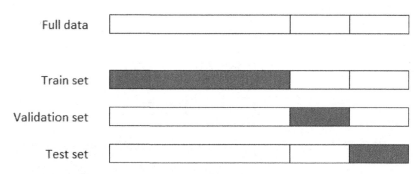

Figure 11.2 – Traditional train/validation/test sets

After the full data has been split, your model is trained on the train set and performance is evaluated on the validation set. A new set of hyperparameters is chosen for the given algorithm and the model is re-trained on the train set and re-evaluated on the validation set. This process is repeated for however many combinations of hyperparameters you want to try.

The set of hyperparameters with the highest performance on the validation set is chosen for the model; the train and validation sets are combined to train a final model, and this final model is evaluated on the test set. This evaluation is then reported as the model's performance.

With this technique, though, only 60% of your full data is available to tune the model. It would be advantageous to use more data for tuning but using smaller validation and testing sets could introduce bias into your model.

To solve this problem, k-fold cross-validation was developed. In k-fold, the data is still randomly shuffled and has a test set split out, maybe 20% again. The remaining 80% of the data is all used for training. This 80% of data is split into *k* sections, with each section called a *fold*. This is what the process looks like with five folds:

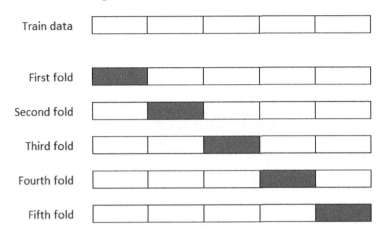

Figure 11.3 – k-fold cross-validation with five folds

For each set of hyperparameters you want to evaluate, you train your model five times. The first time, you set aside the first fold and train on the remaining four. You evaluate on that first fold. You repeat for each fold and take the average of your performance metric across the five folds. Then, you move on to the next set of hyperparameters and repeat.

The process of tuning your hyperparameters takes much longer in this case because of the training for each fold. The advantage, though, is that you are able to use more data for training without introducing bias to your model.

As you know, time series data is sequential and dependent. You cannot shuffle it. You cannot train on future data to predict previous data. This is why both of the methods just demonstrated will not work. We need a way to maintain the order of our data while still setting some aside for testing and validation. That's why forward-chaining was developed.

Performing forward-chaining cross-validation

Forward-chaining cross-validation, also called **rolling-origin cross-validation**, is similar to k-fold but suited to sequential data such as time series. There is no random shuffling of data to begin but a test set may be set aside. The test set must be the final portion of data, so if each fold is going to be 10% of your data (as it would be in 10-fold cross-validation), then your test set will be the final 10% of your date range.

With the remaining data, you choose an initial amount of data to train on, let's say five folds in this example, and then you evaluate on the sixth fold and save that performance metric. You re-train now on the first six folds and evaluate on the seventh. You repeat until all folds are exhausted and again take the average of your performance metric. The folds using this technique would look like this:

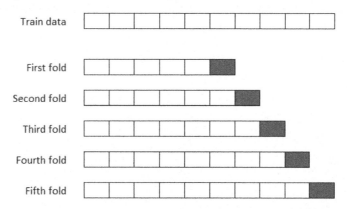

Figure 11.4 – Forward-chaining cross-validation with five folds

In this way, you are able to train your data on sequential data points and evaluate on unseen data, and you are also able to minimize bias by training and testing on a variety of samples.

Prophet has a built-in diagnostics tool for performing forward-chaining cross-validation. Let's now see how to use it with our retail sales dataset.

Creating the Prophet cross-validation DataFrame

To perform cross-validation in Prophet, first you need a fitted model. So, we'll begin with the same procedure we've completed throughout this book. This dataset is very cooperative so we'll be able to use plenty of Prophet's default parameters. We will plot the changepoints, so be sure to include that function with your other imports before loading the data:

```
import pandas as pd
import matplotlib.pyplot as plt
from fbprophet import Prophet
from fbprophet.plot import add_changepoints_to_plot
```

```
df = pd.read_csv('online_retail.csv')
df['date'] = pd.to_datetime(df['date'])
df.columns = ['ds', 'y']
```

This dataset does not have very complicated seasonality, so we'll reduce the Fourier order of yearly seasonality when instantiating our model, but keep everything else default, before fitting, predicting, and plotting. We'll use a 1-year future forecast:

```
model = Prophet(yearly_seasonality=4)
model.fit(df)
future = model.make_future_dataframe(periods=365)
forecast = model.predict(future)
fig = model.plot(forecast)
add_changepoints_to_plot(fig.gca(), model, forecast)
plt.show()
```

As expected, this plot shows the same data as *Figure 11.1* where the data was introduced. There were no significant trend changepoints identified and a very gently sloping upward trend. There appears to be a mild increase in sales during the summer but a dramatic increase over the winter holiday season, as can be seen in the following plot:

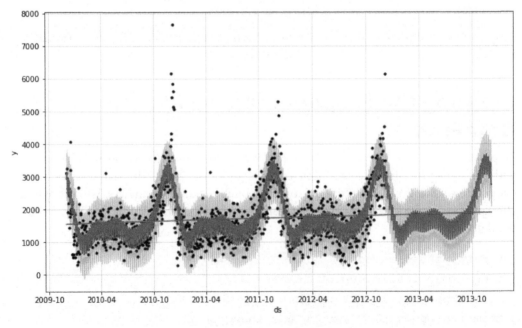

Figure 11.5 – Online retail sales forecast

Let's plot the components now to better understand our seasonalities:

```
fig2 = model.plot_components(forecast)
plt.show()
```

The `trend`, `weekly` seasonality, and `yearly` seasonality show clear patterns:

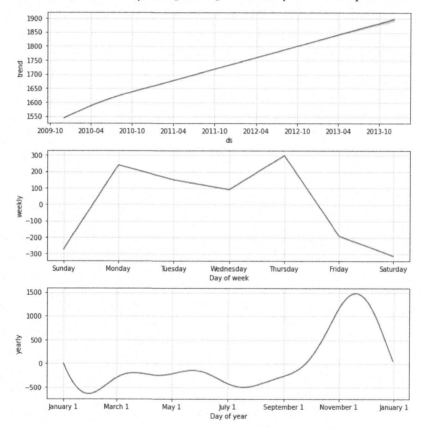

Figure 11.6 – Online retail sales components plot

As we predicted, the `yearly` seasonality reflects that winter spike. As I mentioned when introducing this data, the retailer largely caters to wholesalers, not consumers. So, their purchasing occurs during the business week far more than the weekends. `Friday` sales are even down compared with the rest of the week.

Now, let's perform the actual cross-validation. To do that, we first need to import the function from Prophet's `diagnostics` package:

```
from fbprophet.diagnostics import cross_validation
```

Before we see how to use that function, there are some terms we need to discuss:

- `initial` is the first training period. In *Figure 11.5*, it would be the first five blocks of data in the first fold. It is the minimum amount of data needed to begin your training on.

- `horizon` is the length of time you want to evaluate your forecast over. Let's say that this retail outlet is building their model so that they can predict sales over the next month. A horizon set to 30 days would make sense here, so that they are evaluating their model on the same parameter setting that they wish to use it on.

- `period` is the amount of time between each fold. It can be either greater than the horizon or less than it, or even equal to it.

- `cutoffs` are the dates where each horizon will begin.

This vocabulary is illustrated here:

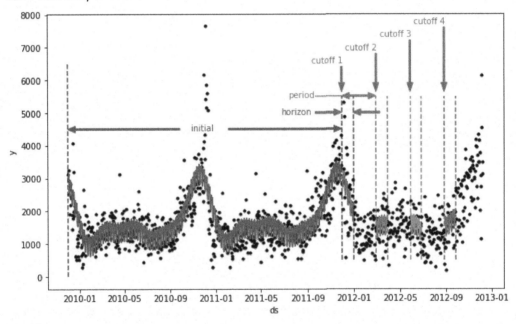

Figure 11.7 – Cross-validation terminology

For each `cutoff`, the model would be trained on all data up to that `cutoff`, and then a prediction will be made for the `horizon` period. That prediction will be compared to the known values and evaluated. Then, the model will be re-trained on all data up to the second `cutoff` and the process will be repeated. The final performance evaluation will be the average of the performance at each cutoff.

Let's imagine that this retail outlet wants a model that is able to predict the next month of daily sales, and they plan on running the model at the beginning of each quarter. They have 3 years of data and want (as is recommended for Prophet) at least two full cycles of seasonality, which because they are modeling yearly seasonality will be 2 years.

They would set their initial training data to be 2 years, then. They want to predict the next month of sales, and so would set `horizon` to 30 days. They plan to run the model each business quarter, and so would set the period to be 90 days. That's what was shown previously in *Figure 11.7*. Now let's apply this to Prophet.

The `cross_validation` function takes two required arguments, the fitted model and `horizon`. Also, `period` and `initial` can be stated, but they are not required. If left at their defaults, `period` is half of `horizon` and `initial` will be three times `horizon`. The output of the function is the cross-validation DataFrame. Let's create this DataFrame and call it `df_cv`:

```
df_cv = cross_validation(model,
                         horizon='90 days',
                         period='30 days',
                         initial='730 days')
```

Each of the `horizon`, `period`, and `initial` arguments takes a string with a style compatible with pandas' `Timedelta` format, for example, `'5 days'`, `'3 hours'`, or `'10 seconds'`. In this example, we're switching the `horizon` and `period` values from those shown in *Figure 11.7*. The retail outlet wants to predict 3 months of daily sales and update their predictions every month (this is probably a more realistic use of the forecast; these parameters are reversed in the image merely to avoid overlapping the horizons to keep the image clear).

We begin our training with an initial period of 2 years, which is `'730 days'`. We set `horizon='90 days'` to evaluate our forecast over a 90-day prediction interval. And finally, we set `period='30 days'`, so we re-train and re-evaluate our model every 30 days. This results in a total of 10 forecasts to compare with the final year of data.

You may also specify the `cutoff` values, but this is usually unnecessary. However, we'll cover a specific instance in *Chapter 12, Performance Metrics*, where you will want to set them yourself. Prophet's default behavior is to set them automatically by working backward from the end of the timeseries.

Now, let's take a look at this DataFrame by displaying the first five rows:

```
df_cv.head()
```

If you run that code in a Jupyter Notebook, you'll see the following formatted output (your values for `yhat_lower` and `yhat_upper` may slightly differ due to randomness in the optimization algorithms):

	ds	yhat	yhat_lower	yhat_upper	y	cutoff
0	2011-12-15	2801.207224	2108.388270	3494.372655	3702.986147	2011-12-14
1	2011-12-16	2352.337392	1618.069152	3030.804134	1229.263629	2011-12-14
2	2011-12-17	2182.401681	1456.391411	2881.701806	1325.415023	2011-12-14
3	2011-12-18	2165.497675	1487.607958	2873.287167	2739.454215	2011-12-14
4	2011-12-19	2636.183079	1947.967823	3315.979099	2699.823386	2011-12-14

Figure 11.8 – The cross-validation DataFrame

For each unique `cutoff` in the DataFrame, you will find 90 days in the `ds` column, corresponding to the 90-day horizon. Each date in `ds` has the true value `y`, which is the same value from your training data, `df['y']`, and the value forecast in that fold for that date, in the `yhat` column.

Note that this is a different `yhat` from that in the `forecast` DataFrame, as those values were calculated with the full dataset, not with a cross-validated fold. The cross-validation DataFrame also contains uncertainty intervals for these forecasts, in `yhat_upper` and `yhat_lower`.

This DataFrame allows you to compare forecasted values with actual values across the range of datetime values in your data. In the `forecast` DataFrame, all `yhat` values for dates in the future obviously have no true `y` value to compare with. For dates in the history, there is a corresponding `df['y']` value to compare your `forecast['yhat']` value with, but the forecast was trained on this value. The `forecast['yhat']` values are biased, whereas the `df_cv['yhat']` values are unbiased and therefore will provide a more accurate representation of what you can expect your model to predict on new, unseen data.

Parallelizing cross-validation

There is a lot of iteration going on during cross-validation and these are tasks that can be parallelized to speed things up. All you need to do to take advantage of this is use the `parallel` keyword. There are four options you may choose: `None`, `'processes'`, `'threads'`, or `'dask'`:

```
df_cv = cross_validation(model,
                         horizon='90 days',
```

```
                        period='30 days',
                        initial='730 days',
                        parallel='processes')
```

Setting `parallel='processes'` uses Python's `concurrent.futures.`
`ProcessPoolExecutor` class, whereas `parallel='threads'` uses `concurrent.`
`futures.ThreadPoolExecutor`. If you're unsure which of these to use, go with
`'processes'`. It will give the best performance on a single machine.

`None` will perform no parallelism, which can be good if you plan to do other work on
your machine while Prophet calculates and you don't want Prophet to take up all of your
machine's resources. If using `'dask'`, you will need to install Dask separately and use
`dask.distributed Client` to connect to the cluster (the following code will result
in an error if Dask has not been separately installed and setup):

```
from dask.distributed import Client


client = Client()
df_cv = cross_validation(model,
                         horizon='90 days',
                         period='30 days',
                         initial='730 days',
                         parallel='dask')
```

Although you can use Dask on your laptop, its power really comes into effect when using
multiple computing clusters across many machines. If you don't have access to this type of
computing power, `parallel='processes'` will usually be the faster option.

Summary

We began this chapter with a discussion of why k-fold cross-validation was developed in
traditional machine learning applications, and we then learned why it will not work with
time series. You then learned about forward-chaining, also called rolling-origin cross-
validation, for use with time series data.

You learned the keywords of initial, horizon, period, and cutoffs, which are used to define
your cross-validation parameters, and you learned how to implement them in Prophet.
Finally, you learned the different options Prophet has for parallelization, in order to speed
up model evaluation.

These techniques provide you with a statistically robust way to evaluate and compare models. By isolating the data used in training and testing, you remove any bias in the process and can be more certain that your model will perform well when making new predictions about the future.

In the next chapter, you'll apply what you learned here to measure your model's performance and tune it for optimal results.

12
Performance Metrics

No model of a real-world phenomenon is perfect. There are countless statistical assumptions made about the underlying data, there is noise in the measurements, and there are unknown and unmodeled contributing factors to the output. But even though it is not perfect, a good model is still informative and valuable. So, how do you know whether you have such a good model? How can you be sure your predictions for the future can be trusted? **Cross-validation** got us part of the way there, by providing a technique to compare unbiased predictions to actual values. This chapter is all about how to compare different models.

Prophet features several different metrics that are used for comparing your actual values with your predicted values, so you can quantify the performance of your model. This tells you how good your model actually is and whether you can trust the predictions, and helps you compare the performance of different models so you can choose which one is best.

This chapter will teach you about the following:

- Understanding Prophet's metrics
- Creating the Prophet performance metrics DataFrame
- Handling irregular cut-offs
- Tuning hyperparameters with grid search

Technical requirements

The data files and code for examples in this chapter can be found at
`https://github.com/PacktPublishing/Forecasting-Time-Series-Data-with-Facebook-Prophet`.

Understanding Prophet's metrics

Prophet's `diagnostics` package provides six different metrics you can use to evaluate your model. Those metrics are mean squared error, root mean squared error, mean absolute error, mean absolute percent error, median absolute percent error, and coverage. We'll discuss each of these in turn.

Mean squared error

Mean squared error (**MSE**) is the sum of the squared difference between each predicted value and the actual value, as can be seen in the following equation:

$$\frac{1}{n} \sum_{i=1}^{n} (y_i - \breve{y}_i)^2$$

Figure 12.1 – Mean squared error

The number of samples is represented in the preceding equation with n, while y is an actual value and $\hat{y}$ a forecasted value.

MSE may be the most used performance metric, but it does have its downside. Because it is not scaled to the data, its value is not easy to interpret – the unit of MSE is the square of your y unit. It is also sensitive to outliers, although this may be either desirable or undesirable, depending upon your data and interpretation.

However, it remains popular because it can be proven that MSE is equal to the bias squared plus the variance, so minimizing this metric can reduce both bias and variance. MSE is never negative and the closer it is to zero, the better the model.

Root mean squared error

If you scale MSE to the same units as that of your data by taking the square root, you arrive at the **root mean squared error** (**RMSE**):

$$\sqrt{\frac{1}{n}\sum_{i=1}^{n}(y_i - \check{y}_i)^2}$$

Figure 12.2 – Root mean squared error

RMSE shares the same advantages and disadvantages as MSE, although its units are more interpretable. As with MSE, it places more importance on the points with large errors than those with small errors.

Mean absolute error

Mean absolute error (**MAE**) is similar to MSE except that it takes the absolute value of the error, not the square:

$$\frac{1}{n}\sum_{i=1}^{n}|y_i - \check{y}_i|$$

Figure 12.3 – Mean absolute error

MAE, in contrast with MSE and RMSE, weighs each error equally; it does not place more importance on outliers or points with uncommonly high error. Like MSE though, MAE is not scaled to the data. So, if you find that your model reports an MAE of, say, 10, is this good or bad? If the average value in your dataset is 1,000, then an error of 10 would be just 1%. If the average of your data is 1, though, then an MAE of 10 would mean your predictions are off by 1,000%!

In order to scale MAE to the data, it will often be divided by the data's mean value, to arrive at a percentage:

$$\frac{\frac{1}{n}\sum_{i=1}^{n}|y_i - \check{y}_i|}{\bar{y}}$$

Figure 12.4 – Mean absolute error (percent)

This format for MAE is not supported in Prophet, although you can create it yourself.

Mean absolute percent error

Mean absolute percent error (**MAPE**) is another very common metric despite its poor ability to represent performance of a model. Not to be confused with total MAE divided by the mean value, MAPE divides each error by the value of the data point at that error:

$$\frac{1}{n} \sum_{i=1}^{n} \left| \frac{y_i - \check{y}_i}{y_i} \right|$$

Figure 12.5 – Mean absolute percent error

This makes the metric skewed to overly represent errors that occur when the data values are low. Optimizing for MAPE will often leave your model undershooting the values it is targeting. Furthermore, because you are dividing by each y-value, if any of them are zero then the calculation will produce a division-by-zero error. Very small values of y will also cause floating-point calculation problems. Prophet will detect whether any y-values are at or near to zero and if found, it will simply skip MAPE calculations and proceed to the other metrics called for. The upside to MAPE, though, is that it has natural interpretability – it is easy to intuitively understand.

Median absolute percent error

Prophet also includes **median absolute percent error** (**MdAPE**), but only in Python as of version 0.71. MdAPE is the same as MAPE, except it uses the median instead of the mean. It can be useful with noisy data, when MAPE may be the preferred metric but too many outliers are swaying it. For example, significant holidays can create large spikes in data and the median would be better able to smooth out predictions if MAPE experiences issues.

Coverage

The final Prophet metric is **coverage**. Coverage is simply the percentage of actual values that lie between the predicted upper and lower uncertainty bounds. By default, the uncertainty limits cover 80% of the data, so your coverage value should be 0.8.

If you find a coverage value that does not equal the `interval_width` set during model instantiation, it means your model is not well calibrated to the uncertainty. In practice, this simply means that you probably cannot trust the stated uncertainty intervals in the future portions of your forecast and may want to adjust them based upon the coverage value.

And of course, the cross-validation DataFrame contains all of your actual y values and your model's predicted $\hat{y}$ values, so any other metric you can come up with to compare those values, you can calculate and use yourself.

Choosing the best metric

Deciding which performance metric to optimize your model for is not a trivial choice. It can have a significant impact on your final model, depending upon the characteristics of the data. As it works out mathematically, it can be shown that optimizing your model for MSE will create a model predicting values close to the mean of your data, and optimizing for MAE will create predictions close to the median value. Optimizing for MAPE will tend to produce abnormally low forecasts because it applies such a high weight to errors occurring at low points in the data.

So, between MSE (or RMSE) and MAE, which is better? RMSE aims to be correct on the average data point and MAE aims to overshoot the actual value as often as it undershoots. This difference will only materialize when the mean and median of your data are different – in highly skewed data. As the median will be further from the tail in skewed data than the mean will be, the MAE will introduce bias toward the bulk of data and away from the tail. A biased model is the greatest disadvantage of MAE.

MSE's disadvantage is its sensitivity to outliers. Imagine a time series that is generally flat except for a couple of extreme outliers. MSE will really focus in on the forecast errors at those outliers, and so it will tend to miss the mark more often than MAE will. In general, the median is more robust to outliers than the mean is.

So, should we consider robustness to outliers a good thing? Not necessarily. If your time series is intermittent – that is, if most dates have a y-value of 0 – you don't want to target the median value but the mean. The median will be 0! In this case, you would desire MSE precisely because it is sensitive to the outliers.

Unfortunately, there is no easy answer to which is the best metric to use. The analyst must pay attention to bias, skewness, and outliers to determine which metric will work best. And there is no reason you can't try multiple metrics and see which forecast seems the most reasonable to you!

Creating the Prophet performance metrics DataFrame

Now that you've learned what the different options are for performance metrics in Prophet, let's start coding and see how to access these. We'll use the same online retail sales data we used in *Chapter 11, Cross-Validation*. Along with our usual imports, we are going to add the `performance_metrics` function from Prophet's `diagnostics` package and the `plot_cross_validation_metric` function from the `plot` package:

```
import pandas as pd
import matplotlib.pyplot as plt
from fbprophet import Prophet
from fbprophet.plot import add_changepoints_to_plot
from fbprophet.diagnostics import cross_validation
from fbprophet.diagnostics import performance_metrics
from fbprophet.plot import plot_cross_validation_metric
```

Next, let's load the data, create our forecast, and plot the results:

```
df = pd.read_csv('online_retail.csv')
df.columns = ['ds', 'y']

model = Prophet(yearly_seasonality=4)
model.fit(df)
forecast = model.predict()
fig = model.plot(forecast)
add_changepoints_to_plot(fig.gca(), model, forecast)
plt.show()
```

Because we're not interested in any future predictions, we don't need to create the `future` DataFrame. We'll just focus on the 3 years of data we've got:

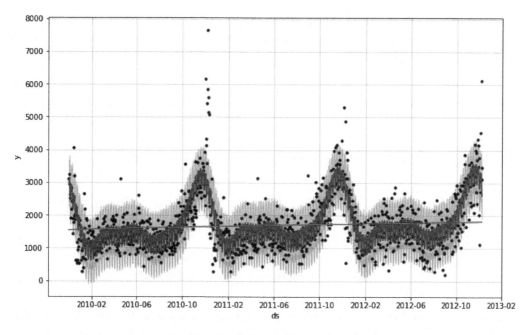

Figure 12.6 – Online retail sales forecast

The performance_metrics function requires a cross-validation DataFrame as input, so we'll create one in the same manner as you learned in *Chapter 11, Cross-Validation*. We'll set horizon to 90 days, so each fold in the cross-validation will be 90 days. The period of 30 days is how often to begin a new fold and initial of 730 days is our first 2-year training period, untouched by validation:

```
df_cv = cross_validation(model,
                         horizon='90 days',
                         period='30 days',
                         initial='730 days',
                         parallel='processes')
```

Next, we'll send df_cv to the performance_metrics function. By default, this function will calculate each of the five available metrics. You can specify a subset of these by passing a list of metric names to the metrics argument. Let's include all five and display the first few rows of the resulting DataFrame:

```
df_p = performance_metrics(df_cv)
df_p.head()
```

The output DataFrame is indexed by days in the `horizon`, so each row represents the values of those metrics when the model is asked to forecast that many days out. This is just the first five rows (your results may vary slightly due to randomness in the optimization algorithm):

	horizon	mse	rmse	mae	mape	mdape	coverage
0	9 days	221414.637261	470.547168	379.222017	0.300342	0.230643	0.855556
1	10 days	217886.528127	466.783170	374.813252	0.297143	0.223107	0.855556
2	11 days	202750.966319	450.278765	368.159469	0.287512	0.204026	0.877778
3	12 days	178915.164185	422.983645	350.389468	0.273400	0.209786	0.911111
4	13 days	172812.883168	415.707690	344.207267	0.260578	0.190466	0.922222

Figure 12.7 – Performance metrics DataFrame

You may be wondering why the first row in the `horizon` column is 9 days. Each metric value in the DataFrame is the rolling average of its calculation up to the day specified. The `performance_metrics` function takes a `rolling_window` argument where you can change the window size, but the default is 0.1. This number is the fraction of `horizon` to include in the window. With 10% of our 90-day `horizon` being 9 days, this is the first row of the DataFrame.

You can use this DataFrame on its own or you can visualize it with Prophet's `plot_cross_validation_metric` function. This function actually calls the `performance_metrics` function itself, so you do not need to create a `df_p` first, just a `df_cv`. Here, we'll plot the MAE by passing `'mae'` to the `metric` argument:

```
fig = plot_cross_validation_metric(df_cv, metric='mae')
plt.show()
```

The resulting plot shows each MAE measurement along the horizon and the rolling average value of those measurements:

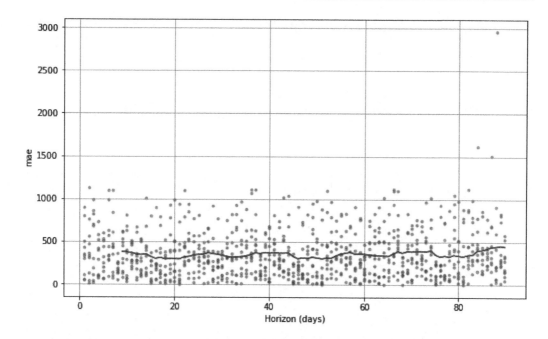

Figure 12.8 – Cross-validation plot

Our cross-validation settings were `horizon='90 days'`, `period='30 days'`, `initial='730 days'`, which, for the 1 year of data remaining after the initial training period, resulted in a total of ten 90-day forecasts. So, for each day in our horizon, the preceding plot will have 10 MAE measurements. If you counted up all the dots on that plot, it should be 900. The solid line is the rolling average value, with the window size being the same default `0.1` as the `performance_metrics` DataFrame.

You can specify this by using the same `rolling_window` argument in the `plot_cross_validation_metric` function. Just to make it very clear how this window size affects the plot, let's compare two RMSE plots, one with a 1% window size and one with a 10% size:

```
fig = plt.figure(figsize=(10, 6))
ax = fig.add_subplot(111)
plot_cross_validation_metric(df_cv,
                             metric='rmse',
                             rolling_window=.01,
                             ax=ax)
plot_cross_validation_metric(df_cv,
                             metric='rmse',
```

```
                              rolling_window=.1,
                              ax=ax)
plt.show()
```

We use the `ax` argument to plot both lines on the same chart:

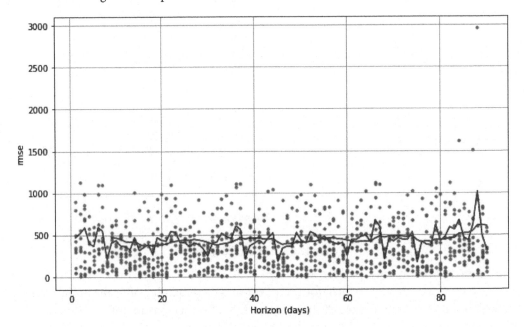

Figure 12.9 – Comparing different window sizes

The smoother line is the one with a wider window size, the default window size. Because the window is not centered but set to the right edge, the first 8 days do not show the rolling average line when using 10% of the horizon. Setting the window to 1% will include all data at the cost of being noisier.

Now that you've learned how to use the cross-validation plot, let's use it to see a problem that can arise when letting Prophet automatically select the cut-off dates to begin each cross-validation fold.

Handling irregular cut-offs

We'll be using a new dataset for this example. The **World Food Programme (WFP)** is the branch of the United Nations focused on hunger and food security. One of the greatest contributing factors to food security issues in developing countries that the WFP tracks is rainfall amounts because it can affect agricultural production. Thus, predicting rainfall is of critical importance in planning aid delivery.

This data represents the rainfall received over 30 years in one of the regions the WFP monitors. What makes this dataset unique is that the WFP recorded the amount of rain that accumulated at three times per month, on the 1st, the 11th, and the 21st. The accumulation from the 1st to the 11th is a 10-day period. It's the same with the 11th to the 21st. But the period from the 21st of one month to the 1st of the next varies depending upon the month. In a normal February, it will be 8 days. In a leap year, 9 days. Months of 30 and 31 days will see a period of 10 and 11 days respectively.

Let's perform cross-validation as you've learned so far and see what effect this will have. First, we need to train a Prophet model on the data. You should have everything already imported if you're continuing from the previous example:

```
df = pd.read_csv('rainfall.csv')
df.columns = ['ds', 'y']


model = Prophet(yearly_seasonality=4)
model.fit(df)
future = model.make_future_dataframe(periods=365 * 5)
future = future[future['ds'].dt.day.isin([1, 11, 21])]
forecast = model.predict(future)
fig = model.plot(forecast)
a = add_changepoints_to_plot(fig.gca(), model, forecast)
plt.show()
```

If you remember, cross-validation is not concerned with any future, unknown periods. Therefore, it's unnecessary to build a `future` DataFrame and predict on it. I did so in this example merely to remind you of the first potential pitfall you learned about in *Chapter 3, Non-Daily Data*, when we used data with regular gaps. We needed to adjust our `future` DataFrame to avoid unconstrained predictions, and we've done that again here by restricting future dates only to those on the 1st, 11th, and 21st of each month. Here's what the forecast looks like:

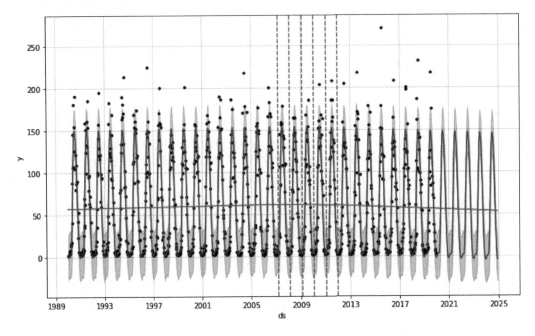

Figure 12.10 – Rainfall forecast

It has a nearly flat trend, rising slightly until 2010 and then turning downward. As you may have expected, the model is dominated by yearly seasonality, with rainfall in December (summer in the Southern Hemisphere) at almost zero and rainfall at its maximum in June.

Now let's build a cross-validation plot. We'll forecast `90 days` (the horizon) and create a new fold every `30 days` (the period). Our initial training period will be `1826 days`, or 5 years. Finally, let's plot RMSE:

```
df_cv = cross_validation(model,
                        horizon='90 days',
                        period='30 days',
                        initial='1826 days',
```

```
                      parallel='processes')
df_p = performance_metrics(df_cv)
fig = plot_cross_validation_metric(df_cv, metric='rmse')
plt.show()
```

Prophet uses the `horizon`, `period`, and `initial` to calculate a set of evenly spaced cut-offs. The `horizon` is then used again to set the length of each fold's forecast but `period` and `initial` are not needed after choosing the cut-offs.

The effect of letting Prophet automatically set the cut-offs is that they are inconveniently located compared to our data. We only have data for 3 days per month, and those 3 days are not consistently spaced. This means that each fold in our cross-validation starts effectively randomly somewhere in the data, producing a plot that seems to suggest each day in the horizon has data:

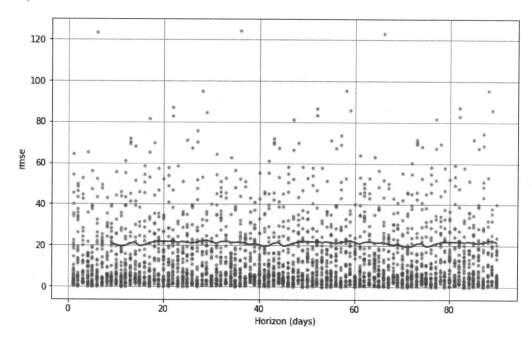

Figure 12.11 – Cross-validation with automatic cut-offs

The `cross_validation` function will accept a `cutoffs` argument that takes a list of user-specified cut-off dates to use. This also means that `initial` and `period` are no longer necessary. This code block will use a list comprehension to iterate over each year, then each month, then each day of either the 1st, 11th, or 21st, and create a list of pandas `Timestamps`:

```
cutoffs = [pd.Timestamp('{}-{}-{}'.format(year, month,
                                          day))
           for year in range(2005, 2019)
           for month in range(1, 13)
           for day in [1, 11, 21]]
```

Now, if we replot our cross-validation but send this list of cut-off dates, we'll see something dramatically different:

```
df_cv = cross_validation(model,
                         horizon='90 days',
                         parallel='processes',
                         cutoffs=cutoffs)
df_p = performance_metrics(df_cv)
fig = plot_cross_validation_metric(df_cv, metric='rmse')
plt.show()
```

Now, each fold is begun on a day for which we have data. The next day for which data exists will be either 8, 9, 10, or 11 days later. Hence, the plot shows 4 discrete days in `horizon` where a forecast took place:

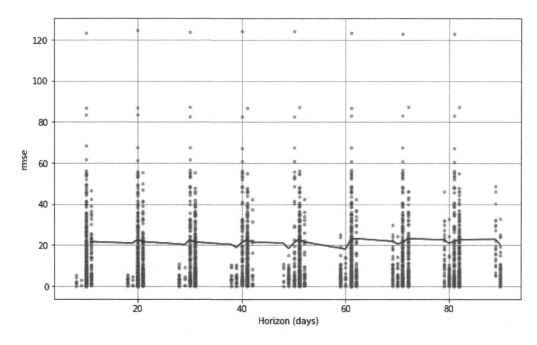

Figure 12.12 – Cross-validation with custom cut-offs

Both *Figure 12.11* and *Figure 12.12* show an average RMSE of just above 20, so the results are very similar. The difference is simply ease of interpretation and consistency. You may encounter this situation often if your data is recorded monthly or in any increment of months because they have inconsistent durations.

Tuning hyperparameters with grid search

For the final section in this chapter, we'll look at grid search and work through an example, continuing with this rainfall data. If you're not familiar with the concept of grid search, it's a way to exhaustively check all reasonable combinations of hyperparameters against a performance indicator and choose the best combination to train your final model. With Prophet, you might decide to select the following hyperparameters and values:

changepoint_prior_scale	seasonality_prior_scale	holidays_prior_scale	seasonality_mode
0.5	10	10	'additive'
0.1	1	1	'multiplicative'
0.01	0.1	0.1	
0.001	0.01	0.01	

Figure 12.13 – Prophet grid search parameters

With these parameters, a grid search will iterate through each unique combination, use cross-validation to calculate and save a performance metric, and then output the set of parameter values which resulted in the best performance.

Prophet does not have a grid search method the way, for example, sklearn does. One is easy enough to build yourself in Python though, so let's see how to set it up. The first step is to define our parameter grid. We'll use the grid shown in *Figure 12.13*, but we're not including holidays in our model (the weather doesn't regularly check its calendar and adjust rainfall if it finds a holiday!), so we'll leave that out:

```
param_grid = {'changepoint_prior_scale': [0.5, 0.1, 0.01,
                                          0.001],
             'seasonality_prior_scale': [10.0, 1.0, 0.1,
                                         0.01],
             'seasonality_mode': ['additive',
                                  'multiplicative']}
```

Next, we'll use Python's itertools package to iterate over that grid and create a list of each unique combination. We'll need to import itertools first; and while we're at it, let's import numpy as well, because we'll be using it later. We'll also create an empty list to hold all of the RMSE values, assuming that's our chosen performance metric:

```
import numpy as np
import itertools


all_params = [dict(zip(param_grid.keys(), value))
              for value in itertools.product(
                               *param_grid.values())]
rmse_values= []
```

We could allow Prophet to define our cut-off periods, but because we're using this rainfall data, let's set the cutoffs ourselves:

```
cutoffs = [pd.Timestamp('{}-{}-{}'.format(year, month,
                                          day))
           for year in range(2010, 2019)
           for month in range(1, 13)
           for day in [1, 11, 21]]
```

The final step in running our grid search, before we evaluate the results, is to iterate over each combination we saved in the `all_params` list, and build a model, a cross-validation DataFrame, and a performance metrics DataFrame.

Let's say that we know we want `yearly_seasonality=4` to keep the curve smooth, and we'll complete model instantiation with the parameter combination for that iteration. In the `performance_metrics` function, we are using `rolling_window=1`. This means that we are averaging 100% of the data in that fold to calculate the metric, so instead of a series of values, we only get one:

```
for params in all_params:
    model = Prophet(yearly_seasonality=4, **params).fit(df)
    df_cv = cross_validation(model,
                             cutoffs=cutoffs,
                             horizon='30 days',
                             parallel='processes')
    df_p = performance_metrics(df_cv, rolling_window=1)
    rmse_values.append(df_p['rmse'].values[0])
```

That code is going to take a long time to run. The length of our `all_params` list, after all, is 32, which means you'll be training and cross-validating 32 total models. I did say grid search was exhaustive! (On a typical laptop, you can expect it will take around 8-12 hours to complete; to speed up the example, you may consider reducing the number of parameters in the `param_grid` dictionary, such as for example: `param_grid = {'changepoint_prior_scale': [0.1, 0.01], 'seasonality_prior_scale': [1.0, 0.1]}`, which will train and cross-validate only four total models. Be sure to recreate your `all_params` dictionary after changing the `param_grid`.) To inspect the results, we'll build a DataFrame with the parameter combinations and their associated RMSEs, and then display a portion of it:

```
results = pd.DataFrame(all_params)
results['rmse'] = rmse_values
results.head()
```

The full DataFrame has 32 rows, one for each combination of parameters, but here we see the first five rows:

	changepoint_prior_scale	seasonality_prior_scale	seasonality_mode	rmse
0	0.5	10.0	additive	22.621225
1	0.5	10.0	multiplicative	23.044739
2	0.5	1.0	additive	22.622803
3	0.5	1.0	multiplicative	23.054798
4	0.5	0.1	additive	22.631216

Figure 12.14 – Grid search DataFrame

Finally, let's use NumPy to find the parameters with the lowest RMSE value and then print them:

```
best_params = all_params[np.argmin(rmse_values)]
print(best_params)
```

Printing those best_params should display this output:

```
"'changepoint_prior_scale': 0.01,
 'seasonality_prior_scale': 1.0,
 'seasonality_mode': 'additive'}
```

The biggest difference between the best parameters found with grid search and those we've used so far is that the changepoint regularization would be better set to a much stronger level. With a lower prior scale, the magnitudes of changepoints would be less, and the trend curve would be even flatter. Intuitively, this seems appropriate; especially for longer forecasts, where allowing larger trend changes would create unrealistic rainfall forecasts far into the future.

Probably the most critical parameter to tune is changepoint_prior_scale. If this value is too small, the trend will underfit the variance. Variance that should be modeled with the trend will instead be modeled in the noise term. If the prior scale is too large, the trend will exhibit too much flexibility and may start to capture some of the yearly seasonality. A range between 0.5 and 0.001 will work in most cases.

The seasonality_prior_scale is probably the second-most impactful parameter. A typical range is usually 10, with essentially no regularization, down to 0.01. Anything smaller and the seasonality is likely to be regularized to a negligible effect. You also have the option of setting each seasonality to False and using add_seasonality to choose prior scales individually, but this causes your grid search to increase in computing time exponentially.

You may also want to add the `fourier_order` to your grid search, but I've found it works great to build a quick model with defaults, inspect the components, and choose Fourier orders myself that fit my intuition. In a fully automated setup, keeping Fourier orders at their defaults will probably be fine.

The `holidays_prior_scale` is also a tunable parameter, with many of the same characteristics as `seasonality_prior_scale`. Just keep in mind that many models won't have holidays and so there would be no need to include this parameter.

The last of the *critical parameters* that should always be considered is the `seasonality_mode`. In this book, you learned a few rules-of-thumb to help decide which mode to use, but more often than not, it isn't clear. The best thing to do is simply inspect a plot of your time series and see whether the magnitude of seasonal fluctuations grows with the trend or stays constant. If you can't tell, go ahead and add `seasonality_mode` to the grid.

Usually, the default value of 80% for `changepoint_range` will be good. It provides a nice balance of allowing the trend to change where appropriate but not allowing it to overfit in the last 20% of data where errors cannot be corrected. If you're the analyst and paying close attention, it's easy to see if the default range is not appropriate. But in a fully automated setting, it's probably better to be conservative and leave it at 80%.

The remaining parameters are best left out of your grid search. For `'growth'`, it is either `'linear'`, `'logistic'`, or `'flat'`, and you as the analyst should choose. Setting it to `'logistic'` will require setting a `'cap'` and `'floor'` as well. For many of the remaining parameters, such as `n_changepoints` and the yearly, weekly, and daily seasonalities, these are better controlled with parameters already included in the search: `changepoint_prior_scale` in the case of changepoints and `seasonality_prior_scale` with seasonalities.

For the final parameters, `mcmc_samples`, `interval_width`, and `uncertainty_samples`, these don't affect your yhat in any way and therefore have no effect on your performance metric. They only control the uncertainty intervals.

Use common sense with grid search – it is a very long process, so don't include each parameter and every possible value in your hyperparameter grid. Often the best approach an analyst can take is to provide intuition and human sense to the process and let the computer do the number crunching.

Summary

In this chapter, you learned how to use Prophet's performance metrics to extend the usefulness of cross-validation. You learned about the six metrics Prophet has out of the box, namely mean squared error, root mean squared error, mean absolute error, mean absolute percent error, median absolute percent error, and coverage. You learned many of the advantages and disadvantages of these metrics, and situations where you may want to use or avoid any one of them.

Next, you learned how to create Prophet's performance metrics DataFrame and use it to create a plot of your preferred cross-validation metric so as to be able to evaluate the performance of your model on unseen data across a range of forecast horizons. You then used this plot with the World Food Programme's rainfall data to see a situation where Prophet's automatic cut-off date selection is not ideal, and how to create custom cut-off dates.

Finally, you brought all of this together in an exhaustive grid search of Prophet hyperparameters. This process enabled you to use a data-driven technique to finely tune your model and optimize it for a metric of your choice.

In the next chapter, the final chapter of this book, you will learn a few more tricks in Prophet's bag to help put your models into a production environment.

13
Productionalizing Prophet

If you have made it through all of the chapters in this book, congratulations! You are well prepared to take on any forecasting assignments Prophet can handle. This final chapter will cover a few additional features that can be helpful in a production environment.

In this chapter, you'll learn how to save a trained model for reuse later and you'll learn how you can speed up model fitting when new data becomes available. To close out the chapter, you'll discover a new series of interactive plots that can be used in a web dashboard to share your work with a wider audience. The topics covered in this chapter will be the following:

- Saving a model
- Updating a fitted model
- Making interactive plots with Plotly

Technical requirements

The data files and code for the examples in this chapter can be found at `https://github.com/PacktPublishing/Forecasting-Time-Series-Data-with-Facebook-Prophet`.

Saving a model

In *Chapter 10, Uncertainty Intervals*, you forecasted the number of crimes per day in the city of Baltimore, using **Markov chain Monte Carlo (MCMC)** sampling. This was a long computation, and you were only using daily data. Had you used the Divvy hourly data instead, a dataset more than 10 times larger, the computation would have been even longer. And these two datasets are certainly smaller than many you'll encounter in the real world. If Prophet provided no way to save your work, every time you trained a model, you would have to leave the model in your computer's memory for as long as you wanted to use it.

Maybe you're familiar with the `pickle` module in Python—this works great to save your trained models in `sklearn`, for example. However, Prophet uses Stan in the backend to build its models and these Stan objects don't pickle well. Fortunately, Prophet includes some functions to serialize your model in JSON and re-open it later. So, once your model is trained, you can put it away for the day and bring it back later whenever you want to predict a future date.

We'll use the Baltimore crime data again to see how to save your model. We'll need to import `pandas` in order to read the `csv` file; Prophet, of course, to build our model; and we'll also need to import `json` to save and reopen the file. The functions to convert a model object into JSON and back again are imported from Prophet's `serialize` package:

```
import pandas as pd
from fbprophet import Prophet
import json
from fbprophet.serialize import model_to_json, \
model_from_json
```

Now, we'll run through the now-familiar process of opening our data and training a model. We're also discarding the outliers from the data, as we did in *Chapter 10, Uncertainty Intervals*:

```
df = pd.read_csv('baltimore_crime.csv')
df.columns = ['ds', 'y']
df.loc[df['y'] > 250, 'y'] = None

model = Prophet()
model.fit(df)
```

We've now got our trained model. Previously, you would have needed to keep your Python kernel running and the model in memory for as long as you wanted to access it. At the end of the day, you would want to save it, shut down your machine, and go home for the night, but you would lose all that work.

In the following code, you'll use the `with` statement to create a context manager so that you can open a JSON file, and Python will automatically close it when you're done. The `'w'` and `'r'` arguments used in the following statements merely stand for *write* and *read*. This code block uses Prophet's `model_to_json` function to convert the `model` object into a JSON file, and then it saves it to your hard drive:

```
with open('baltimore_crime_model.json', 'w') as file_out:
    json.dump(model_to_json(model), file_out)
```

Now that the file is saved, you can safely shut down Python. To convert the JSON file back into a `model` object, simply use the `json_to_model` function:

```
with open('baltimore_crime_model.json', 'r') as file_in:
    model = model_from_json(json.load(file_in))
```

With the model reloaded, you can use it just as you would any fitted model; for example, you can plot a forecast:

```
forecast = model.predict()
fig = model.plot(forecast)
```

With no `future` created, this is just the fitted model:

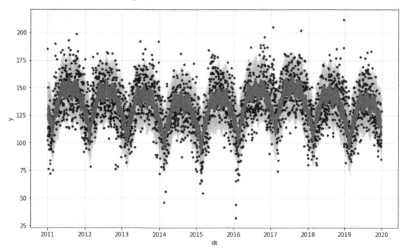

Figure 13.1 – Baltimore crime forecast

Saving and re-opening your work can certainly be helpful, but the real value is when you keep a model around and every day update it with new data, as we'll do next.

Updating a fitted model

Forecasting is unique among predictive models in that the value of the data is its recency and each passing moment creates a new set of valuable data to use. A common situation with a forecast model is the need to refit it as more data comes in. The city of Baltimore, for example, may use the crime model to predict how many crimes they might expect to happen tomorrow, so as to better place their officers in advance. Once tomorrow arrives, they can record the actual data, retrain their model, and predict for the next day.

Prophet is unable to handle online data, which means it cannot add a single new data observation and quickly update the model. Prophet must be trained offline—the new observation will be added to the existing data and the model will be completely retrained. But it doesn't have to be completely retrained from scratch and the following technique will save a lot of time when retraining.

Prophet is essentially an optimization problem. Deep in the code are some settings to pick a set of initial parameters that Prophet believes will be close to the actual parameters needed to model the forecast curve. It then creates its curve, measures the error with existing data points, updates the parameters to reduce the error, and repeats.

Many hundreds or thousands of iterations may occur as Prophet attempts to get closer and closer to the best set of parameters. You can greatly speed up this optimization problem by taking the already-optimized parameters from yesterday's model and using them as better initializations for today's model. The assumption is that today's data point will not dramatically change the overall model, which is generally a very good assumption. Let's see how this technique works.

We'll begin by creating a DataFrame of the Baltimore crime data with the final observation removed. This is *yesterday's* data:

```
df_yesterday = df[df['ds'] < df['ds'].max()]
```

Now, we'll fit `model1` on this data:

```
model1 = Prophet().fit(df_yesterday)
```

The city of Baltimore could use this model to make a prediction about the next day's activity, for example. Now, let's say that the next day has arrived; we record the day's crime level and want to update our model with df, *today's* data, which has that final data point included. Let's first do it from scratch and use the IPython timeit magic function to see how long it takes:

```
%timeit model2 = Prophet().fit(df)
```

On my current machine as I write this, the process took about 865 milliseconds according to the output:

```
865 ms ± 183 ms per loop (mean ± std. dev. of 7 runs, \
                      1 loop each)
```

Now, let's do it again, but instead of starting from scratch, we'll give Prophet a *warm-start* by passing it the parameters from yesterday's model for initialization. We first need to define a class to format those parameters correctly:

```
import numpy as np


class StanInit:
    def __init__(self, model):
        self.params = {
            'k': np.mean(model.params['k']),
            'm': np.mean(model.params['m']),
            'sigma_obs': \
            np.mean(model.params['sigma_obs']),
            'delta': np.mean(model.params['delta'],
                            axis=0),
            'beta': np.mean(model.params['beta'], axis=0)
        }
    def __call__(self):
        return self.params
```

This class simply opens up the model.params dictionary and saves the relevant values into a new dictionary formatted as the Stan backend requires. We now use this class to extract the parameters from model1 and pass this initialization to the fit method, again timing the process:

```
%timeit model2 = Prophet().fit(df, init=StanInit(model1))
```

When I run that command, I see more than a 4x improvement in training speed:

```
195 ms ± 90 ms per loop (mean ± std. dev. of 7 runs, \
                    1 loop each)
```

0.195 seconds compared to 0.865 seconds is a dramatic improvement. The amount of time saved depends on many factors and will often vary even when you repeat the experiment again.

There is one caveat with this method though: if the locations of changepoints change, the updated model may actually take *longer* to fit than just fitting from scratch. For these reasons, this method works best when adding a very small amount of new data relative to the existing data, like we did here by adding one day to several years of data.

With MAP estimation, as we just did in the previous example, each iteration is an optimization problem. This means that better initialization will speed things up considerably. With MCMC sampling, however, each iteration must fully run through each link in the Markov chain (refer back to *Chapter 10, Uncertainty Intervals*, for a review of the difference between MAP estimation and MCMC sampling).

What this means is that warm-starting will speed up MAP estimation considerably but will not speed up MCMC sampling. Warm-starting will, however, increase the quality of each Markov chain iteration. So, if you do a warm-start with MCMC sampling, you can probably get away with fewer `mcmc_samples` without a significant reduction in result quality.

This reduction in `mcmc_samples` creates an opportunity to speed up MCMC sampling on any new model. The idea is to train an initial model with MAP estimation, and then use that model to warm-start a model with MCMC sampling, but using fewer `mcmc_samples` than you would otherwise choose:

```
model1 = Prophet().fit(df)
model2 = \
Prophet(mcmc_samples=200).fit(df,init=StanInit(model1))
```

In the preceding code block, we created an initial `model1` using MAP estimation and all data. We then used the parameters from `model1` to warm-start `model2`, which uses MCMC sampling, but only `mcmc_samples=200`, instead of the value of `300` we chose in *Chapter 10, Uncertainty Intervals*. This will result in an MCMC-sampled model with roughly the same performance as earlier but trained in two-thirds of the time.

In summary, warm-starting with MAP estimation (that is, when `mcmc_samples=0`) will speed up your model training. Warm-starting will not speed up a model when `mcmc_samples` is greater than 0 though, but in this case, you can quickly train a model with MAP estimation and then warm-start your model with `mcmc_samples` set to a reduced value, without losing much quality. Now, let's learn how to use Prophet to make interactive plots.

Making interactive plots with Plotly

In this final section, we'll use the Plotly library to build some interactive plots. **Plotly** is a completely separate visualization package to the **Matplotlib** package, which we've been using throughout this book. A plot made with Plotly is richly interactive, allowing tooltips on mouse hover, zooming in and out of a plot, and all sorts of other interactivities.

If you're familiar with Tableau or Power BI, Plotly brings similar interactivity to Python. Additionally, the Plotly team also built **Dash**, a library for creating web-based dashboards. A full tutorial for creating such a dashboard is beyond the scope of this book, but I encourage you to learn this valuable tool if you would like to share your Prophet forecasts with a wide audience.

Prophet does not automatically install Plotly as a dependency, so before we begin, you will need to install it on your machine. It is a simple process and can be accomplished through either `conda` or `pip`. Here is the `conda` installation command:

```
conda install -c plotly plotly=4.14.3
```

If you have not installed Anaconda or Miniconda though, you will have to use `pip`:

```
pip install plotly==4.14.3
```

If you tend to work in Jupyter Notebook or JupyterLab, you will also want to install some support packages. This can be done through `conda`, as shown here:

```
# Jupyter Notebook support
conda install "notebook>=5.3" "ipywidgets>=7.5"
# JupyterLab support
conda install jupyterlab "ipywidgets>=7.5"
# JupyterLab renderer support
jupyter labextension install jupyterlab-plotly@4.14.3
# OPTIONAL: Jupyter widgets extension
jupyter labextension install @jupyter-widgets/jupyterlab-\
manager plotlywidget@4.14.3
```

If you do not have `conda`, you may also use `pip` instead:

```
# Jupyter Notebook support
pip install "notebook>=5.3" "ipywidgets>=7.5"
# JupyterLab support
pip install jupyterlab "ipywidgets>=7.5"
# JupyterLab renderer support
jupyter labextension install jupyterlab-plotly@4.14.3
# OPTIONAL: Jupyter widgets extension
jupyter labextension install @jupyter-widgets/jupyterlab-\
manager plotlywidget@4.14.3
```

If you have trouble with any of these commands, the best resource is Plotly's own documentation: `https://plotly.com/python/getting-started/`.

You have already learned about many of the plotting functions in Prophet's `plot` package throughout the examples in this book. There are four functions that we haven't touched on yet; these take many of the same keywords as the Matplotlib counterparts you have learned already but output a Plotly chart instead.

> **Important note**
>
> This book will contain static images of Plotly plots, but if you run the example code in a Jupyter Notebook, you'll be able to manipulate the image in a richly interactive environment.

To demonstrate these tools, let's use the Divvy data again, and use temperature as an extra regressor. We won't be using Matplotlib at all in this section, so no need to import it. We've already got `pandas` and Prophet imported from the previous sections, but we'll need to make a few more imports here.

If you recall from *Chapter 8, Additional Regressors*, we artificially reduced our training data by 2 weeks so that we could forecast 2 weeks ahead while using weather as additional regressors. We'll do that again here, and so we need to import `timedelta` to help out. Most importantly though, we'll import `plotly.offline` and initialize notebook mode:

```
from datetime import timedelta
import plotly.offline as py
py.init_notebook_mode()
```

Now, let's read in our data and put it into a DataFrame. We'll only use one additional regressor in this example, `temperature`:

```
df = pd.read_csv('divvy_daily.csv')
df = df[['date', 'rides', 'temperature']]
df['date'] = pd.to_datetime(df['date'])
df.columns = ['ds', 'y', 'temp']
```

Finally, we just build our model as before. We create a regressor for temperature, then fit the model on the data while excluding the final 2 weeks. We next make a future forecast of 2 weeks, using those unfitted 2 weeks of `temperature` data in the `future` DataFrame:

```
model = Prophet(seasonality_mode='multiplicative',
                yearly_seasonality=6)
model.add_regressor('temp')

model.fit(df[df['ds'] < df['ds'].max() - \
          timedelta(weeks=2)])

future = model.make_future_dataframe(periods=14)
future['temp'] = df['temp']
forecast = model.predict(future)
```

So far, this should all be review (except for importing and initializing Plotly). But now, we'll import those final four functions from the `plot` package:

```
from fbprophet.plot import (
    plot_plotly,
    plot_components_plotly,
    plot_forecast_component_plotly,
    plot_seasonality_plotly
)
```

Plotly forecast plot

Let's run through these one by one. First up is `plot_plotly`. To use this function, you simply pass in the model and the forecast. I'm also including the `trend=True` argument to include the trend line in the plot. You could also add `changepoints=True`, and it would completely mimic the `add_changepoints_to_plot` Matplotlib function. The `py.iplot(fig)` line is analogous to Matplotlib's `plt.show()`:

```
fig = plot_plotly(model, forecast, trend=True)
py.iplot(fig)
```

This screenshot also displays the tooltip shown on hover over the point for **May 10, 2015**:

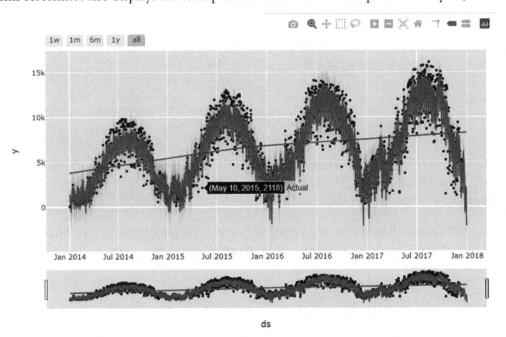

Figure 13.2 – Plotly plot

Plotly components plot

Next up, we'll look at the Plotly components plot. This is much the same as the Matplotlib version, but it also includes interactivity. I'm also including the `figsize` argument to reduce the size of this one a bit:

```
fig = plot_components_plotly(model, forecast ,
                             figsize=(800, 175))
py.iplot(fig)
```

This plot shows the same subplots as `plot_components`:

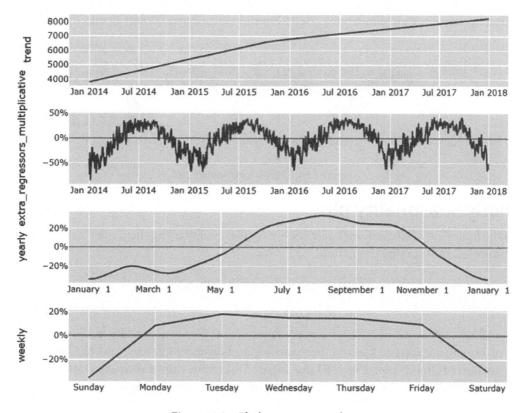

Figure 13.3 – Plotly components plot

Plotly single component plot

I wanted to use this Divvy data so that we could use the temperature extra regressor. We could have plotted any of the subplots in *Figure 13.3* using this next function, but all of them can be handled with other functions, except for extra regressors. Plotting those alone requires the use of the `plot_forecast_components_plotly` function. Here, we pass in the `'temp'` component:

```
fig = plot_forecast_component_plotly(model, forecast,
                                      'temp')
py.iplot(fig)
```

As with the other plots in this section, a static image does not do them justice. Plotly was intended to be used in an interactive environment; these plots beg to be placed in a dashboard, not printed in a book. Here, I'm showing a hover tooltip again:

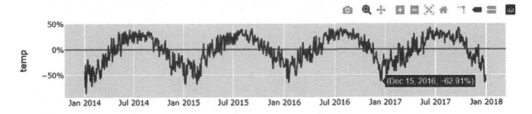

Figure 13.4 – Plotly temperature plot

Plotly seasonality plot

In the final Plotly function, we'll plot the yearly seasonality using the `plot_seasonality_plotly` function:

```
fig = plot_seasonality_plotly(model, 'yearly')
py.iplot(fig)
```

The Plotly toolbar has been left out of the components plot to save space but is included in all the others; you can see it in the upper right of *Figures 13.2, 13.4*, and *13.5*. In the following seasonality plot, I've used the **Toggle Spike Lines** and **Compare Data** buttons from this toolbar to add further information to the hover tooltip, seen here:

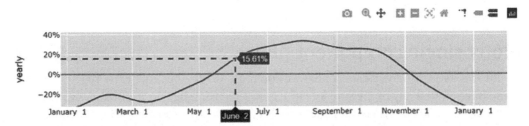

Figure 13.5 – Plotly seasonality plot

I strongly encourage you to explore these plots in a Jupyter notebook, and if you find them useful, consider putting them together in a dashboard using Dash. There are plenty of tutorials available online.

Summary

This last chapter in the book was the most optional of all of them, but for those of you who often work in a production environment, these tools will be invaluable.

In this chapter, you learned how to save a model to your hard drive using JSON serialization, so you can share it or open it up later without requiring the model to be retrained. You also learned how to update a model that has already been fitted, another procedure designed to save you time. Finally, you examined a new plot format, an impressive tool to make your plots interactive in a browser, and hopefully, you saw the potential of packaging this information into a dashboard.

Together, what you learned in this chapter will help you to update your model as time progresses and new data comes in, and share that model via live, web-based interactive dashboards.

Packt.com

Subscribe to our online digital library for full access to over 7,000 books and videos, as well as industry leading tools to help you plan your personal development and advance your career. For more information, please visit our website.

Why subscribe?

- Spend less time learning and more time coding with practical eBooks and Videos from over 4,000 industry professionals

- Improve your learning with Skill Plans built especially for you

- Get a free eBook or video every month

- Fully searchable for easy access to vital information

- Copy and paste, print, and bookmark content

Did you know that Packt offers eBook versions of every book published, with PDF and ePub files available? You can upgrade to the eBook version at packt.com and as a print book customer, you are entitled to a discount on the eBook copy. Get in touch with us at customercare@packtpub.com for more details.

At www.packt.com, you can also read a collection of free technical articles, sign up for a range of free newsletters, and receive exclusive discounts and offers on Packt books and eBooks.

Other Books You May Enjoy

If you enjoyed this book, you may be interested in these other books by Packt:

Hands-On Time Series Analysis with R

Rami Krispin

ISBN: 978-1-78862-915-7

- Visualize time-series data and derive useful insights
- Study auto-correlation and understand statistical techniques
- Use time-series analysis tools from the stats, TSstudio, and forecast packages
- Explore and identify seasonal and correlation patterns
- Work with different time-series formats in R
- Discover time-series models such as ARIMA, Holt-Winters, and more
- Evaluate high-performance forecasting solutions

Packt is searching for authors like you

If you're interested in becoming an author for Packt, please visit `authors.packtpub.com` and apply today. We have worked with thousands of developers and tech professionals, just like you, to help them share their insight with the global tech community. You can make a general application, apply for a specific hot topic that we are recruiting an author for, or submit your own idea.

Leave a review - let other readers know what you think

Please share your thoughts on this book with others by leaving a review on the site that you bought it from. If you purchased the book from Amazon, please leave us an honest review on this book's Amazon page. This is vital so that other potential readers can see and use your unbiased opinion to make purchasing decisions, we can understand what our customers think about our products, and our authors can see your feedback on the title that they have worked with Packt to create. It will only take a few minutes of your time, but is valuable to other potential customers, our authors, and Packt. Thank you!

Index

Made in the USA
Coppell, TX
10 October 2021